A FIELD GUIDE

LIFE SKILLS FOR TEEN BOYS WITH ADHD

110 Step-by-Step Skills for Focus, Organization, Money, Friendships, and Independence

AGES 13 TO 18

RICHARD BASS

For boys who think fast and forget faster.

Disclaimer: This book is for informational and educational purposes only. It is not a substitute for professional medical, psychological, educational, or legal advice, diagnosis, or treatment. Always seek the guidance of a qualified health provider with any questions regarding a medical or mental health condition. Never disregard professional advice or delay seeking it because of something you have read here.

First edition, 2026.

THIS PAGE IS FOR THE GROWN UP

BEFORE YOU HAND IT OVER

Thank you for buying this. Here is the part that decides whether it works.

> **And if you are the teenager and you read this page anyway:** good. Now you know exactly what I told them. Nothing on this page is behind your back.

Do not present it. A book handed over with a speech about how this could really help you becomes evidence in an old argument before it is ever opened. Leave it on his bed, or in the stack of Christmas things, and say nothing.

Do not ask if he has read it. Not next week, not next month. Asking turns it into an assignment, and he already has enough of those.

Expect it to be used out of order. It is built for that. If he reads eleven pages and uses two of them, the book worked.

If he wants to talk about one, follow his lead. Do not use it as a way into the other nine things you have been meaning to bring up. He will notice, and the book will close.

One last thing. A few pages talk plainly about money, driving, anger, and alcohol. The alcohol page does not assume he is drinking and does not treat it as inevitable. It says the answer is no until he is of legal age, and then it gives him the one thing nobody tells boys with ADHD: that alcohol hits impulse control first, and impulse control is already the system he has the least of to spare. He is going to meet that information eventually. I would rather he met it here, from someone who is not handing him a drink.

THIS BOOK BELONGS TO

FROM

BECAUSE

SOMEBODY GAVE YOU THIS

And you did not ask for it. Somebody who loves you bought a book about your brain and left it somewhere you would find it, which is either sweet or deeply annoying depending on the hour.

So let us get the awkward part out of the way.

This is not a book about fixing you. Nobody is going to tell you to try harder. If trying harder worked, it would have worked by now, roughly nine hundred attempts ago.

Here is what is actually true. You are running a brain built for interesting, not for important. Those are different things, and school, jobs, parents, deadlines, and the DMV all care about the second one. Almost nothing that matters is also interesting. That is the entire problem, in one sentence, and it is not a personality defect.

YOU ARE NOT BAD AT LIFE.
YOU ARE RUNNING DIFFERENT HARDWARE.

What follows is a hundred and ten workarounds. Some of them are so simple they will feel stupid. Those are the ones that survive a bad week, so try them anyway.

You do not have to read this. You do not have to tell anyone you read this. Steal four ideas and let the rest sit on a shelf looking like you read it.

Four is plenty.

THE SIX MOVES

There are a hundred and ten skills in this book and only six ideas underneath them. Once you spot the six, you can build your own skills for situations nobody wrote a page about.

01 GET IT OUT OF YOUR HEAD

Working memory is a small counter. Paper, calendars, and lists are a bigger one.

02 SHRINK THE FIRST STEP

Starting is the wall, not finishing. Make the first move insultingly small.

03 BUILD IN A DELAY

Your first impulse is loud and usually wrong. Put twenty minutes between it and you.

04 CHANGE THE ROOM

Willpower loses to environments. Move the phone, not your intention

05 SAY IT EARLY AND SHORT

Silence is what turns a small problem into a broken thing. Short beats explained.

06 BORROW OUTSIDE STRUCTURE

Attach the new thing to a person, a place, or something you already do without deciding.

Every skill page is tagged with the moves it uses. If one move keeps working for you, the index on page 135 lists every skill that runs on it.

CONTENTS

03 PEOPLE

04 TAKING CARE OF YOUR BODY AND YOUR HEAD

05 HANDLING WHAT COMES NEXT

HOW TO USE THIS BOOK

Do not read this front to back. Seriously. It is not built that way and you will not finish it, and then you will feel bad about a book, which is a stupid thing to feel bad about.

Every skill is one page, and every page has the same four parts in the same order. Learn the shape once and you never have to hunt.

The ten second version is the whole skill in one line. If you read nothing else on the page, read that. It is genuinely enough. This is not a trick to get you to read the rest.

Why this is harder for you is what your brain is actually doing. Not an excuse. A problem you understand is much easier to beat than one you think is a personal flaw.

Do this is the steps. Small enough to start today.

If it goes sideways is for when it does not work the first time, which it will not, for everyone, always.

Use the Find It Fast index in the back when you know how you feel but not what you need.

> **About the phone instructions:** a few pages name exact menus, like Settings, Accessibility, Color Filters. Phone companies move those around every year or two just to keep everyone humble. If a path does not match your screen, open Settings and use the search bar at the top. The feature is still there. It moved.

WHAT IS ACTUALLY GOING ON

Ninety seconds on the machinery. Then we never do science again.

THE NAME IS WRONG

It is not a shortage of attention. You have plenty. It goes where it wants instead of where you point it, which is a steering problem, not a fuel problem.

NOW VERSUS LATER

Your brain runs on two settings, now and not now. A deadline three weeks out lives in not now, where it cannot be felt, until the night it moves to now and becomes a crisis.

THE START BUTTON

Knowing what to do and being able to start are separate systems. Yours are wired further apart than most. That gap is where try harder lands uselessly.

WORKING MEMORY

The mental countertop where you hold four instructions is smaller. Not weaker, smaller. That is why step three vanished and why writing things down is not a crutch, it is a bigger counter.

FEELINGS ARRIVE LOUD

Emotions land at higher volume and take longer to fade. A flat text can feel like a door slammed. Knowing that is happening does not stop it, but it buys you twenty minutes of not sending anything.

HYPERFOCUS

The same wiring that loses your keys can lock onto something for six hours and produce work nobody else in the room could have done. It is not a consolation prize. It is the actual upside.

EVERY SKILL IN HERE IS BUILT FOR THAT MACHINE.

PART ONE OF FIVE

01
RUNNING YOUR OWN LIFE

You are not bad at life. You are running a brain built for interesting, not for important. Those are different things, and school and jobs and parents mostly care about the second one.

That gap is where things fall apart. Not because you do not care. Because caring does not turn into starting on its own.

This part closes the gap with systems, not willpower. Systems work on the days motivation does not show up.

01 HOW TO GET OUT THE DOOR ON TIME

MOVE 03 · BUILD IN A DELAY	MOVE 04 · CHANGE THE ROOM

THE TEN SECOND VERSION

Everything by the door the night before. Set an alarm labeled leave now, and leave.

WHY THIS IS HARDER FOR YOU

Your brain does not measure time in minutes. It measures it in not yet and oh no. The shower feels like five minutes and takes twenty.

You also lose a chunk of every morning searching for things, and nobody builds that into their estimate. **Fix the searching and you fix the mornings.**

DO THIS

1. **The night before, stage everything by the door.** Backpack, shoes, keys, charger, water bottle.
2. **Lay out your clothes too.** This removes a decision from a moment when you are bad at decisions.
3. **Set two alarms.** One to get up, one twenty minutes later that means you should be dressed by now.
4. **Set a third alarm labeled leave now,** ten minutes before you actually have to go.
5. **When that alarm goes off, go.** Whatever you were about to do, do not do it.

IF IT GOES SIDEWAYS

If you keep getting pulled into one more thing on the way out, know that there is never one more thing. There are eleven.

02 HOW TO START HOMEWORK WHEN YOUR BRAIN SAYS NO

MOVE 02 · SHRINK THE FIRST STEP

THE TEN SECOND VERSION

Set a ten minute timer, phone in another room, easiest question first.

WHY THIS IS HARDER FOR YOU

Starting is the hardest part, and it is a real neurological thing, not laziness. Your brain wants a reward it can see, and a worksheet due Thursday offers nothing.

So you wait until panic shows up, because panic is the only chemical strong enough to launch you. **You can start without panic.** It just takes a smaller ask.

DO THIS

1. **Set a timer for ten minutes.** Not an hour. Ten.
2. **Put your phone in a different room.** Face down on the desk does not work and you know it.
3. **Do the easiest question first,** even if it is out of order. You are buying momentum, not being efficient.
4. **When the timer goes off, decide: stop or keep going.** Both are allowed. Usually you keep going, because starting was the wall.
5. **Write one sentence about where you stopped.** Future you has no memory of this moment.

IF IT GOES SIDEWAYS

If ten minutes feels impossible, do three. Three minutes of started beats sixty minutes of planning to start.

03 HOW TO STOP LOSING YOUR KEYS, WALLET, AND PHONE

MOVE 04 · CHANGE THE ROOM

THE TEN SECOND VERSION

One spot by the door. Empty your pockets into it before you do anything else.

WHY THIS IS HARDER FOR YOU

You do not lose things because you are careless. You set them down while thinking about something else, so the moment never got recorded. There is no memory to search.

That is why retracing your steps rarely works for you. **The fix is not remembering better.** The fix is removing the decision of where to put it.

DO THIS

1. **Pick one spot near the door.** A bowl, a hook, a tray. One spot, not twc
2. **Everything that leaves the house with you lives there** when you are home.
3. **Empty your pockets into it the second you walk in.** Before food, before phone, before sitting down.
4. **Do it for two weeks even when it feels pointless.** It goes automatic around day ten.
5. **Give your phone its own charging spot,** and make it the same spot every night.

> IF IT GOES SIDEWAYS
>
> *If you keep walking past the spot, move the spot. It should be somewhere you physically cannot avoid, not around a corner.*

04 HOW TO BREAK A HUGE ASSIGNMENT INTO PIECES YOU WILL ACTUALLY START

MOVE 02 · SHRINK THE FIRST STEP

MOVE 01 · GET IT OUT OF YOUR HEAD

THE TEN SECOND VERSION

Write every action, not every topic. Break anything over thirty minutes. Start with the easiest.

WHY THIS IS HARDER FOR YOU

A big project shows up in your head as one enormous blob labeled PROJECT. Blobs cannot be started. There is no first move, so your brain avoids the whole thing.

Your job is to turn the blob into a list of steps so small they feel almost insulting. Insultingly small is the point.

DO THIS

1. **Write the assignment at the top of a page.** Leave the rest blank.
2. **List every single thing that has to happen.** Not chapters. Actions. Find three sources. Read source one. Write the first paragraph.
3. **Break anything longer than thirty minutes** into smaller pieces.
4. **Circle the easiest item on the list.** That is your first move, even if it is not the logical first step.
5. **Do it and physically cross it off.** Seeing progress is fuel for your brain specifically.

> IF IT GOES SIDEWAYS
>
> *If you cannot figure out the steps, you do not understand the assignment yet. Asking the teacher is a step. Put it on the list.*

05 HOW TO USE A CALENDAR THAT SURVIVES REAL LIFE

MOVE 01 · GET IT OUT OF YOUR HEAD

THE TEN SECOND VERSION

One calendar. Appointments and deadlines only. Add a start date three days before every due date.

WHY THIS IS HARDER FOR YOU

Most people use a calendar to remember. You need one to think for you, because out of sight means genuinely gone.

The problem is that elaborate systems collapse in about nine days, and then you decide calendars do not work for you. **Simple survives. Complicated does not.**

DO THIS

1. **Pick one calendar and only one.** The one on your phone is fine. Not an app and a planner and a whiteboard.
2. **Put in only two kinds of things:** appointments with a time, and deadlines with a due date.
3. **For every deadline, add a second entry three days earlier** that says start this. The start date is the useful one.
4. **Turn on two notifications for every entry:** one at twenty four hours before, and one at sixty minutes before. One alert is never enough for you.
5. **Check it at the same moment every day,** attached to something you already do without fail, like eating breakfast.

IF IT GOES SIDEWAYS

If you stop checking it for a week, do not build a new system. Open the same calendar and add today. You took a week off. The system did not fail.

06 HOW TO REMEMBER SOMETHING WITHOUT WRITING IT DOWN BADLY

MOVE 01 · GET IT OUT OF YOUR HEAD

THE TEN SECOND VERSION

One capture spot. Write it as an action the moment it occurs to you.

WHY THIS IS HARDER FOR YOU

You have written things down before. On a receipt, in a note you never opened again, on your hand. The writing was never the problem.

The finding it later was. One place beats a good memory.

DO THIS

1. **Pick one capture spot.** One notes app or one small notebook. Everything goes there.
2. **Write it immediately, however messy.** Do not wait until you are somewhere convenient. You will not remember by then.
3. **Write it as an action, not a topic.** Email Coach Ruiz about Friday, not coach.
4. **Once a day, move anything with a date onto your calendar.**
5. **Cross finished items off instead of deleting them.** A list of done things is worth more to your motivation than a clean list.

IF IT GOES SIDEWAYS

If you find yourself writing in three places again, pick the one you actually open most and move everything there. Do not build a fourth.

07 HOW TO KEEP A ROOM YOU CAN ACTUALLY FIND THINGS IN

MOVE 04 · CHANGE THE ROOM

THE TEN SECOND VERSION

Give every category one home. Reset for ten minutes before bed, not for three hours on Saturday.

WHY THIS IS HARDER FOR YOU

Your room does not get messy in one dramatic collapse. It gets messy one set down object at a time, because putting something away requires deciding where it goes.

Decisions are expensive for you, so you defer them, and deferred decisions pile up on the floor. Fewer decisions, cleaner room.

DO THIS

1. **Sort everything into categories first,** clothes, school, tech, trash. Do not organize yet.
2. **Give each category exactly one home,** and make the home obvious. A bin beats a drawer because you can see into it.
3. **Get rid of anything with no home.** If it does not have a place, it is going to live on the floor.
4. **Set a ten minute timer before bed** and put things back in their homes. Ten minutes daily beats three hours on a Saturday you will never spend.
5. **Keep one open surface permanently clear,** usually your desk. It gives your eyes somewhere to land.

IF IT GOES SIDEWAYS

If a category keeps ending up on the floor, its home is in the wrong place. Move the home closer to where you actually drop the thing.

08 HOW TO ESTIMATE HOW LONG SOMETHING WILL REALLY TAKE

MOVE 01 · GET IT OUT OF YOUR HEAD

THE TEN SECOND VERSION

Guess, then double it. Track three real tasks to find your personal multiplier.

WHY THIS IS HARDER FOR YOU

You are not being optimistic on purpose. Time blindness means you genuinely cannot feel the difference between twenty minutes and ninety, so your guesses are built on nothing.

You cannot fix the feeling, but you can fix the math.

DO THIS

1. **Make your honest guess first** and write it down.
2. **Double it.** That is your working estimate until you have real data.
3. **Time three real tasks this week with your phone's stopwatch,** and write the real number next to your guess. Getting ready and cleaning up both count as part of the task.
4. **Divide real by guess** to find your personal multiplier. Most people land between two and three.
5. **Use your multiplier from now on** instead of doubling by default.

IF IT GOES SIDEWAYS

If you are still late after doubling, you probably forgot the getting started time and the putting away time. Those count.

09 HOW TO HANDLE A SUDDEN SCHEDULE CHANGE WITHOUT LOSING THE DAY

MOVE 02 · SHRINK THE FIRST STEP

THE TEN SECOND VERSION

Name the change out loud, rebuild only the next three hours, and move on.

WHY THIS IS HARDER FOR YOU

A canceled practice or a moved appointment does not just change one block. It knocks over the whole mental structure you built the day on, and rebuilding takes energy you did not budget.

So the day quietly becomes a write off. It does not have to.

DO THIS

1. **Say the change out loud.** Practice is canceled. This sounds silly and it works, because it forces the update to register.
2. **Give yourself five minutes of annoyed.** Not thirty. Set a timer if you need to.
3. **Rebuild only the next three hours,** not the whole day. Three hours is a size your brain can hold.
4. **Pick one thing to do with the freed time** and write it down before you touch your phone.
5. **Start it within ten minutes.** The gap between plan and start is where the day disappears.

IF IT GOES SIDEWAYS

If the day is already gone, salvage one thing. One finished thing changes how tomorrow starts.

10 HOW TO BE THE RELIABLE ONE IN A GROUP PROJECT

MOVE 05 · SAY IT EARLY AND SHORT

THE TEN SECOND VERSION

Claim a specific task early, put the deadline in your calendar, and send updates nobody asked for.

WHY THIS IS HARDER FOR YOU

You may have a history here. Not because you did nothing, but because you did it late, or did the wrong part, or did a great job on something nobody needed.

Reliability in a group is mostly about visibility. People trust what they can see happening.

DO THIS

1. **Volunteer for a specific task in the first meeting,** before the roles get assigned to you.
2. **Pick something with a clear finish line,** like the slides or the data, not something vague like helping out.
3. **Write the due date and a start date into your calendar** before you leave the meeting.
4. **Send a short update halfway through** even though nobody asked. This buys you enormous credit.
5. **Deliver it a day early.** Early is the only version of on time that survives your brain.

IF IT GOES SIDEWAYS

If you fall behind, say so immediately instead of going quiet. Silence is what destroys group trust, not lateness.

11 HOW TO PACK FOR A TRIP WITHOUT FORGETTING SOMETHING IMPORTANT

MOVE 01 · GET IT OUT OF YOUR HEAD

THE TEN SECOND VERSION

Build one reusable list on your phone. Pack from the list, not from memory.

WHY THIS IS HARDER FOR YOU

Packing from memory means walking around a room hoping objects remind you of themselves. Your working memory is not built for that job.

A list is not a sign you are bad at this. It is the tool that makes you good at it.

DO THIS

1. **Make one note on your phone called Packing List** and never delete it.
2. **Write it in categories:** clothes, tech, bathroom, documents, medication.
3. **Pack with the list open,** checking things off as they go into the bag, not after.
4. **Put charger, medication, and ID in the same bag every trip.** Same bag, same pocket, every time.
5. **Add anything you forgot to the list when you get home,** while it still stings.

IF IT GOES SIDEWAYS

If you always forget the same category, put it at the top of the list instead of the bottom. Lists get read from the top down.

12 HOW TO FINISH SOMETHING YOU ARE NINETY PERCENT DONE WITH

MOVE 02 · SHRINK THE FIRST STEP

THE TEN SECOND VERSION

List what is actually left, set a twenty minute timer, and accept good enough.

WHY THIS IS HARDER FOR YOU

The last ten percent is boring, and boring is where your brain checks out. There is no discovery left, only cleanup, so the project sits there almost finished for three weeks.

Almost finished counts as zero to everyone but you.

DO THIS

1. **Write down exactly what is left.** Usually it is smaller than the dread suggests.
2. **Set a twenty minute timer** and do only the items on that list.
3. **Do not improve anything you already finished.** That is avoidance wearing a helpful costume.
4. **Decide what good enough looks like before you start.** Spell it out: spell checked, all questions answered, name on it. Not polished, not impressive. Then stop at that line.
5. **Submit it, send it, or hand it in the same day.** A finished thing on your desk is still unfinished.

IF IT GOES SIDEWAYS

If you cannot face the last ten percent alone, do it next to someone. Another person in the room does most of the work for you.

13 HOW TO FOLLOW MULTI STEP INSTRUCTIONS WITHOUT LOSING STEP THREE

MOVE 01 · GET IT OUT OF YOUR HEAD

THE TEN SECOND VERSION

Write the steps down as you hear them, then repeat them back.

WHY THIS IS HARDER FOR YOU

Someone gives you four instructions and you get two. This is working memory, not attitude, and it is one of the most common reasons people wrongly think you are not listening.

Get it out of your head and onto something you can see.

DO THIS

1. **Pull out your phone or paper before they start talking,** not after.
2. **Write only the verbs.** Call, print, drop off. Fill in details later.
3. **Repeat the list back to them** when they finish. So that is call, print, drop off.
4. **Ask which one is first if the order matters.** People often forget to tell you.
5. **Cross each off as you go,** so you always know where you are.

> IF IT GOES SIDEWAYS
>
> *If someone is talking too fast, say hold on, I want to get this right. Nobody has ever been annoyed by that sentence.*

14 HOW TO STOP READING THE SAME PARAGRAPH SIX TIMES

MOVE 02 · SHRINK THE FIRST STEP

THE TEN SECOND VERSION

Read with a question in mind, move your finger, and summarize out loud every page.

WHY THIS IS HARDER FOR YOU

Your eyes move across text while your attention goes somewhere else entirely, and you do not notice for half a page. Rereading passively just repeats the same failure.

Reading has to become active to hold you.

DO THIS

1. **Turn the heading into a question first.** Read to answer it, not to get through it.
2. **Move your finger or a card under the line** you are on. Physical tracking anchors attention.
3. **Stop at the end of every page and say the point out loud** in one sentence.
4. **If you cannot say it, reread that page only,** not the whole section.
5. **Take a two minute break every fifteen minutes,** and stand up during it.

IF IT GOES SIDEWAYS

If the material is dense, try listening to an audio version while following along in the text. Two channels hold you better than one.

15 HOW TO WAIT WITHOUT LOSING YOUR MINI

MOVE 03 · BUILD IN A DELAY

THE TEN SECOND VERSION

Always carry something to do. Decide what it is before you are stuck.

WHY THIS IS HARDER FOR YOU

Waiting rooms, lines, and bus stops are harder for you than for most people, because your brain treats empty time as an emergency. That is where impulsive scrolling and impulsive spending live.

Plan the waiting instead of enduring it.

DO THIS

1. **Decide before you leave what you will do while waiting.** A podcast, a book, a game.
2. **Keep that thing physically on you,** not at home where it does you no good.
3. **Give your hands something,** a fidget, a pen, a ring. Hands busy makes waiting shorter.
4. **Set a timer if the wait has a known length,** so you stop checking the clock.
5. **Do not open shopping apps while waiting.** This is when your brain buys things.

IF IT GOES SIDEWAYS

If the wait runs long and you feel yourself boiling, go outside and walk to the end of the block and back. Movement resets it.

16 HOW TO SET UP A DESK THAT WORKS FOR YOUR BRAIN

MOVE 04 · CHANGE THE ROOM

THE TEN SECOND VERSION

Face a blank wall, clear the surface, and keep only what the current task needs.

WHY THIS IS HARDER FOR YOU

Everything in your line of sight is competing for your attention, and it is winning more often than it should. A desk facing a window or a doorway is a desk with a hundred interruptions built in.

Design the space so there is less to lose focus to.

DO THIS

1. **Turn the desk to face a wall,** not a window, a TV, or a door.
2. **Clear the surface completely,** then put back only what you use daily.
3. **Keep one drawer or bin for everything else** so clearing takes seconds, not an hour.
4. **Put the charger, headphones, and a pen in fixed spots** so you never hunt for them mid task.
5. **Set out only the materials for the current task** before you sit down.

> IF IT GOES SIDEWAYS
>
> *If you cannot turn the desk, use a large book or a folded piece of cardboard as a temporary wall while you work.*

17 HOW TO USE BODY DOUBLING WITHOUT MAKING IT WEIRD

MOVE 06 · BORROW OUTSIDE STRUCTURE

THE TEN SECOND VERSION

Work next to someone doing their own thing. No talking required.

WHY THIS IS HARDER FOR YOU

Working alongside another person makes hard tasks dramatically easier for a lot of people with ADHD. It is not about being watched. It is about borrowing someone else's momentum.

This is one of the highest return tricks in the book and it costs nothing.

DO THIS

1. **Ask a friend or family member to sit near you** while you both do your own work.
2. **Say the actual ask out loud:** I focus better with someone here, you do not have to talk to me.
3. **Agree on a length up front,** forty five minutes is a good default.
4. **Put both phones out of reach,** or the whole thing turns into hanging out.
5. **If nobody is available, use a library, a coffee shop, or a video call with the mic off.**

IF IT GOES SIDEWAYS

If you end up talking the whole time, sit facing different directions. Same room, different orientation.

18 HOW TO STOP SAYING YES TO EVERYTHING

MOVE 03 · BUILD IN A DELAY

MOVE 05 · SAY IT EARLY AND SHORT

THE TEN SECOND VERSION

Buy time before answering, check your calendar, then answer.

WHY THIS IS HARDER FOR YOU

You say yes because yes feels good right now and the cost lands on a future person you do not have to be yet. Then that person shows up overcommitted and exhausted, and it turns out he is you.

The fix is a delay between the ask and the answer.

DO THIS

1. **Have one sentence ready for every ask:** let me check and get back to you tonight.
2. **Use it even when you are sure the answer is yes.** Especially then.
3. **Look at your actual calendar,** not your sense of how free you feel.
4. **Ask yourself if you would do it tomorrow.** If tomorrow sounds terrible, next month will too.
5. **Answer clearly.** I cannot do it is a complete sentence and needs no essay attached.

> IF IT GOES SIDEWAYS
>
> *If you already said yes and regret it, back out early rather than late. Early is inconvenient. Late is a problem for other people.*

19 HOW TO RECOVER A DAY THAT FELL APART BY NOON

MOVE 02 · SHRINK THE FIRST STEP

THE TEN SECOND VERSION

Stop, eat something, pick one thing, and do it. Do not audit the wreckage.

WHY THIS IS HARDER FOR YOU

The instinct is to spend the afternoon reviewing everything that went wrong, which feels productive and accomplishes nothing except making the evening worse too.

A bad morning does not have to buy the whole day.

DO THIS

1. **Stop and eat something and drink water.** A surprising share of the spiral is physical.
2. **Do not review what went wrong.** That is a tomorrow job, and usually not even that.
3. **Pick one thing that still matters today.** One, not four.
4. **Do it for fifteen minutes,** even badly.
5. **Write one line about what would help tomorrow morning,** then close the day out.

> IF IT GOES SIDEWAYS
>
> *If you cannot pick the one thing, ask what will make tomorrow morning easier. That question usually answers itself.*

20 HOW TO BUILD A ROUTINE THAT STICKS PAST WEEK TWO

MOVE 06 · BORROW OUTSIDE STRUCTURE

THE TEN SECOND VERSION

Attach the new habit to something you already do, and keep it under two minutes at first.

WHY THIS IS HARDER FOR YOU

You have built routines before. Elaborate ones, on a Sunday, with real hope. They died on a Wednesday, and you concluded you are the problem.

You are not. The size was the problem. Routines fail because they are built for your most motivated day.

DO THIS

1. **Pick one habit only.** Not a morning system. One habit.
2. **Shrink it until it takes under two minutes.** Make the bed, not clean the room.
3. **Attach it to something you already do every day** without deciding to, like brushing your teeth.
4. **Do it in the same order every time,** so the first thing pulls the second thing along.
5. **Add a second habit only after the first runs for two weeks** without you thinking about it.

> IF IT GOES SIDEWAYS
>
> *If you miss a day, do it the next day. Missing twice in a row is what actually ends a habit, not missing once.*

21 HOW TO STOP A GAME FROM EATING YOUR ENTIRE SATURDAY

MOVE 03 · BUILD IN A DELAY	MOVE 04 · CHANGE THE ROOM

THE TEN SECOND VERSION

Set the timer before you launch it, and stop at a save point, not at a good stopping point. There is no good stopping point.

WHY THIS IS HARDER FOR YOU

Games are built by teams of very smart adults whose entire job is making sure you do not stop. Every one of them has studied exactly how your reward system works, and they are getting paid well to beat it.

You are not weak. You are outnumbered. Losing to a hundred professionals is not a character flaw, but you still have to fight back with something other than willpower.

DO THIS

1. **Set the alarm before you launch the game,** not once you are in. Once you are in, the version of you who cares about alarms has left the building.
2. **Put the alarm across the room** so turning it off requires standing up. Standing up breaks the spell more than the noise does.
3. **Decide your stopping point in game terms:** after this match, at the next save, end of the round. Just one more is not a stopping point, it is a trapdoor.
4. **Do the thing you owe first, even ten minutes of it.** Games after obligations is a rule you can keep. Games until you feel like stopping is not a rule at all.
5. **Put your phone somewhere else while you play,** or you will lose two things at once and only notice one of them.

> IF IT GOES SIDEWAYS
>
> *If you blow past the alarm every single time, get a friend to play with you who has to log off at a set time. Peer pressure works in both directions and this is the good one.*

22 HOW TO TAKE NOTES YOU WILL ACTUALLY USE LATER

MOVE 01 · GET IT OUT OF YOUR HEAD

THE TEN SECOND VERSION

Fewer words, more structure. Leave a blank margin and fill it in the same day.

WHY THIS IS HARDER FOR YOU

Your notes are either three pages of everything the teacher said or four words and a drawing of a shark. Neither one helps you in April.

Notes are not a transcript, they are a set of handles. You need just enough to pick the memory back up.

DO THIS

1. **Draw a line down the page about a third of the way in.** Notes go on the wide side, nothing goes in the margin yet.
2. **Write only what you would not be able to reconstruct.** Skip anything already on the slides you get to keep.
3. **Star anything the teacher says twice or writes down.** That is the test, announced out loud, for free.
4. **Fill the margin the same day with questions your notes answer.** This takes four minutes and turns them into a study tool instead of a diary.
5. **Photograph the page** if there is any chance the notebook does not survive the week. There is always a chance.

IF IT GOES SIDEWAYS

If you cannot write and listen at the same time, ask to record the class or ask for the slides. Both are normal requests and neither one makes you a lesser student.

PART TWO OF FIVE

02
MONEY AND GETTING INDEPENDENT

Money is where ADHD gets expensive, and not in a small way. Impulse buying, forgotten bills, subscriptions you have not used since ninth

23 HOW TO OPEN YOUR FIRST BANK ACCOUNT

MOVE 04 · CHANGE THE ROOM

THE TEN SECOND VERSION

Bring ID and a parent if you are under eighteen. Ask about fees before you sign.

WHY THIS IS HARDER FOR YOU

Cash disappears from your pocket without leaving a trace, which makes it impossible to learn anything from. An account gives you a record you can look at later.

You need the record more than most people do, because you will not remember where it went.

DO THIS

1. **Pick a credit union or an online bank with no monthly fee, no minimum balance, and a free ATM network.** Credit unions usually beat big banks on all three.
2. **Bring your ID, your Social Security number, and a parent if you are under eighteen.** Under eighteen usually means a joint account.
3. **Ask four questions before you sign:** what fees exist, what happens if I overdraft, is there a debit card, and where can I use an ATM for free.
4. **Turn on a push or text alert for every transaction** before you leave the building. Ask them to set it up with you if you cannot find it.
5. **Open a second savings account at the same time** and give it a name, like Car.

IF IT GOES SIDEWAYS

If a bank pushes overdraft protection, say no for now. It is a fee waiting to happen, and you can add it later.

24 HOW TO BUDGET WHEN YOU SPEND IMPULSIVELY

MOVE 03 · BUILD IN A DELAY

THE TEN SECOND VERSION

Split every dollar you get into three accounts the day it arrives.

WHY THIS IS HARDER FOR YOU

Traditional budgeting asks you to remember a plan at the exact moment your brain is least interested in plans, which is standing in a store wanting something.

Move the money before the moment arrives. A budget you have to remember is not a budget.

DO THIS

1. **The day money comes in, split it immediately.** Do not wait for the weekend.
2. **Send half to spending, thirty percent to saving, twenty percent to a bills account.** Adjust the numbers, keep the structure.
3. **Automate the transfer if your bank allows it,** so it happens without you.
4. **Spend only from the spending account,** and treat the other two as though they do not exist.
5. **Check the balance once a week at the same time,** like Sunday night. Not five times a day and not once a month.

> IF IT GOES SIDEWAYS
>
> *If you keep raiding savings, move it to a different bank so it takes a day to transfer. A day is usually enough delay.*

FULL EXAMPLE ON PAGE 132

25 HOW TO USE THE TWENTY FOUR HOUR RULE

MOVE 03 · BUILD IN A DELAY

THE TEN SECOND VERSION

Put it in the cart, close the app, and decide tomorrow.

WHY THIS IS HARDER FOR YOU

The urge to buy is loudest in the first few minutes and mostly gone by the next day. Advertisers know this, which is why everything is built for instant checkout.

You do not have to fight the urge. You just have to outlast it.

DO THIS

1. **Add the item to the cart or a wish list instead of buying.** This satisfies part of the urge.
2. **Close the app completely.**
3. **Set a reminder for the same time tomorrow** to go look at it again.
4. **Tomorrow, ask where it will be in a month.** In use, or in a drawer.
5. **Buy it if you still want it.** Wanting it a day later is real information.

IF IT GOES SIDEWAYS

For anything over a hundred dollars, use a week instead of a day. Bigger purchase, longer delay.

26 HOW TO STOP PAYING FOR SUBSCRIPTIONS YOU FORGOT ABOUT

MOVE 01 · GET IT OUT OF YOUR HEAD

THE TEN SECOND VERSION

Audit your bank statement once, cancel what you do not use, and set a calendar check every six months.

WHY THIS IS HARDER FOR YOU

Subscriptions are designed for people who forget, which is a category you are firmly in. Nine dollars a month feels like nothing and is over a hundred a year.

This is the easiest money you will ever find.

DO THIS

1. **Open your last two bank or card statements and read every line.** Then check the two places subscriptions hide: on iPhone, Settings, your name, Subscriptions. On Android, the Play Store, your profile icon, Payments and subscriptions.
2. **Write down every recurring charge,** including the ones you forgot existed.
3. **Cancel anything you have not used in a month.** You can resubscribe. That is the whole point of subscriptions.
4. **Put a repeating calendar reminder every six months** called check subscriptions. Set it for a date you will actually be free, like a Sunday.
5. **Before starting any free trial, set a cancel reminder for two days before it ends.**

IF IT GOES SIDEWAYS

If you cannot find how to cancel, search the service name plus cancel subscription. The button is usually hidden on purpose.

27 HOW TO NEVER MISS A BILL PAYMENT

MOVE 06 · BORROW OUTSIDE STRUCTURE

THE TEN SECOND VERSION

Automate everything you can, and put a single bill day on the calendar for the rest.

WHY THIS IS HARDER FOR YOU

Missing a payment is almost never about not having the money. It is about the payment happening on a day you were thinking about something else.

Automation removes your memory from the equation entirely, which is exactly where you want it.

DO THIS

1. **Set autopay on every bill with a fixed amount.** Phone, subscriptions, insurance.
2. **Keep a small cushion in the account autopay pulls from,** so a bad week does not cause an overdraft.
3. **Pick one bill day for anything that cannot be automated,** the same date every month.
4. **Put it on your calendar as a repeating event with a notification.**
5. **Turn on low balance alerts** so you find out before the bank charges you.

IF IT GOES SIDEWAYS

If you overdraft anyway, call and ask them to reverse the fee. First time requests are granted more often than people expect.

28 HOW TO FIND A FIRST JOB

MOVE 02 · SHRINK THE FIRST STEP

THE TEN SECOND VERSION

Apply to ten places in one sitting, in person where possible, and follow up in a week.

WHY THIS IS HARDER FOR YOU

The hardest part of job hunting is that it is many small boring steps with no reward until the end, which is the exact shape of task your brain refuses.

So do it in one concentrated block instead of a little every day. One block you can survive.

DO THIS

1. **Block ninety minutes and apply to ten places in that window.** Do not spread it over two weeks.
2. **Start with places that hire teens constantly:** grocery, food service, retail, movie theaters, camps, warehouses.
3. **Apply in person where you can** and ask for the manager. Showing up beats a form.
4. **Keep a list of where you applied and the date.** You will not remember otherwise.
5. **Follow up once after a week,** in person or by phone. This alone puts you ahead of most applicants.

IF IT GOES SIDEWAYS

If nobody calls back after twenty applications, the problem is usually the resume or the availability you listed. Change one and try again.

29 HOW TO WRITE A RESUME WITH NO WORK EXPERIENCE

MOVE 01 · GET IT OUT OF YOUR HEAD

THE TEN SECOND VERSION

One page. Lead with what you did, not where you did it.

WHY THIS IS HARDER FOR YOU

You have more material than you think. Sports, clubs, volunteering, babysitting, mowing lawns, and school projects are all real evidence that you show up and finish things.

Employers hiring teens are looking for reliability, not experience.

DO THIS

1. **Put your name, phone, and email at the top.** Use an email address that is your actual name.
2. **Write three sections:** experience, activities, skills.
3. **Describe each item with a verb and a number.** Coached two teams of eight kids. Raised four hundred dollars.
4. **List real skills:** languages, software, cash handling, driving, certifications.
5. **Keep it to one page and have one adult read it** before you send it anywhere.

> IF IT GOES SIDEWAYS
>
> *If you have nothing to put in experience, do one volunteer shift this month. One shift gives you a line and a reference.*

FULL EXAMPLE ON PAGE 129

30 HOW TO GET THROUGH A JOB INTERVIEW

MOVE 03 · BUILD IN A DELAY

MOVE 01 · GET IT OUT OF YOUR HEAD

THE TEN SECOND VERSION

Prepare three stories, arrive fifteen minutes early, and ask one question at the end.

WHY THIS IS HARDER FOR YOU

Interviews are hard for you in a specific way. You either go quiet because you are managing yourself, or you talk too much because the silence is unbearable.

Preparation is what keeps you in the middle.

DO THIS

1. **Prepare three short stories before you go:** a time you solved a problem, a time you worked with someone difficult, a time you were reliable.
2. **Arrive fifteen minutes early and sit in the car or outside.** Rushing in wrecks the first two minutes.
3. **Answer, then stop talking.** Count to two in your head before adding anything.
4. **Say you do not know if you do not know,** then say how you would find out.
5. **Ask one question at the end,** like what makes someone good at this job here.

IF IT GOES SIDEWAYS

If you blank completely, say let me think about that for a second. Silence you name is confidence. Silence you fill with noise is not.

FULL EXAMPLE ON PAGE 133

31 HOW TO ASK FOR MORE HOURS OR A RAISI

MOVE 05 · SAY IT EARLY AND SHORT

THE TEN SECOND VERSION

Ask for a specific time to talk, bring evidence, name a number.

WHY THIS IS HARDER FOR YOU

Most people ask at the worst possible moment, in passing, during a rush, with no preparation, and then take the no personally.

The ask is a small meeting, not a conversation you spring on someone.

DO THIS

1. **Ask for five minutes at a slow time,** not mid shift and not on a Friday night.
2. **Write down three specific things you have done** before you go in. Shifts covered, tasks learned, problems solved.
3. **Name what you want out loud.** I would like to move to fifteen dollars, or I would like two more shifts a week.
4. **Stop talking after you ask.** Let the silence sit. This is the hardest and most important part.
5. **If the answer is not now, ask what would need to change and by when.**

> IF IT GOES SIDEWAYS
>
> *If you get a no, do not quit that day. Write the date they gave you in your calendar and ask again then.*

FULL EXAMPLE ON PAGE 134

32 HOW TO READ A PAY STUB

MOVE 01 · GET IT OUT OF YOUR HEAD

THE TEN SECOND VERSION

Check hours, rate, and that gross minus deductions equals what hit your account.

WHY THIS IS HARDER FOR YOU

Payroll mistakes happen more than people admit, and almost nobody checks. Missing hours are common enough that catching one pays for the time it takes to look.

Two minutes a pay period is a real hourly rate.

DO THIS

1. **Find gross pay.** That is before anything comes out.
2. **Check the hours and the rate.** Multiply them yourself and see if it matches.
3. **Look at the deductions:** federal tax, state tax if you have one, Social Security, Medicare.
4. **Find net pay** and confirm that is what actually landed in your account.
5. **If anything is off, tell your manager the same week** with the stub in hand.

IF IT GOES SIDEWAYS

If your check is much smaller than expected, check whether you filled out your tax form correctly when you were hired.

FULL EXAMPLE ON PAGE 131

33 HOW TO BUILD CREDIT WITHOUT WRECKING IT

MOVE 06 · BORROW OUTSIDE STRUCTURE

MOVE 04 · CHANGE THE ROOM

THE TEN SECOND VERSION

One card, one small recurring charge, autopay the full balance every month.

WHY THIS IS HARDER FOR YOU

Credit is a memory test that runs for years, and the penalty for forgetting is expensive and slow to undo. It is also unavoidable if you want an apartment or a car loan later.

Set it up so it runs without you.

DO THIS

1. **At eighteen, get one card only,** a student card or a secured card. Before eighteen, the move is asking a parent to add you as an authorized user, which builds history without putting a card in your hand.
2. **Put one small recurring charge on it,** like a single subscription. Nothing else.
3. **Set autopay for the full statement balance,** not the minimum. The minimum is how debt starts.
4. **Keep your balance under thirty percent of the limit.** On a three hundred dollar limit that means never carrying more than ninety.
5. **Never close your oldest card,** even if you stop using it.
6. **Check your credit report free once a year at annualcreditreport.com,** which is the government authorized site. Anything charging you for a credit report is not the one you want.

IF IT GOES SIDEWAYS

If you cannot trust yourself with the card, freeze it. Literally, in a container of water in the freezer. It still ages and builds history.

34 HOW TO AVOID BUY NOW PAY LATER TRAPS

MOVE 03 · BUILD IN A DELAY

THE TEN SECOND VERSION

Ask if you could pay the full price today. If no, you cannot afford it in four payments either.

WHY THIS IS HARDER FOR YOU

You will not run into this until you are eighteen and have your own account, but it will be waiting for you at every checkout when you get there. Splitting a purchase into four payments is designed to make the price feel smaller, and it works especially well on a brain that struggles to picture future consequences.

The payments do not disappear. They stack, and they arrive on days you forgot about.

DO THIS

1. **Before using it, ask whether you could pay in full today.** If no, do not buy it.
2. **Never run more than one of these at a time.** Two is how people lose track.
3. **Write the payment dates in your calendar** the moment you sign up.
4. **Check the late fee before agreeing,** not after.
5. **Never use it for food, gas, or anything you will consume before it is paid off.**

IF IT GOES SIDEWAYS

If you already have several running, list them all with dates and amounts on one page. Seeing the total is usually the fix.

35 HOW TO SPLIT A BILL WITHOUT IT GETTING WEIRD

MOVE 05 · SAY IT EARLY AND SHORT

THE TEN SECOND VERSION

Say how you are splitting it before the food arrives, and send your share that night.

WHY THIS IS HARDER FOR YOU

The awkwardness is never about the money. It is about the ambiguity, and ambiguity is what makes people avoid each other afterward.

Name the plan early and the whole thing stays easy.

DO THIS

1. **Bring it up before ordering:** separate checks or split even.
2. **If you ordered much less, ask for a separate check up front,** not an adjustment at the end.
3. **Send your share the same night,** before you leave the table if possible.
4. **If you covered someone, say the number once** and then let it go.
5. **If someone owes you and forgot, send the request without a paragraph attached.**

IF IT GOES SIDEWAYS

If someone consistently does not pay you back, stop covering them. Say you are tight this month. That is enough of a reason.

36 HOW TO BUY A USED CAR WITHOUT GETTING BURNED

MOVE 03 · BUILD IN A DELAY

THE TEN SECOND VERSION

Get a mechanic to inspect it before you pay anything, and never buy on the same day you first see it.

WHY THIS IS HARDER FOR YOU

A car is the biggest purchase most teenagers make, and it is bought under exactly the conditions your brain handles worst: excitement, pressure, and a seller who wants a decision today.

Every rule here exists to slow the decision down.

DO THIS

1. **Set your total number first,** including tax, insurance, and registration. Not just the sticker price.
2. **Get an insurance quote before you buy,** because on some cars it costs more than the payment.
3. **Pay a mechanic for a pre purchase inspection,** which runs about one hundred to two hundred dollars. A seller who refuses one is telling you something, and you should walk.
4. **Test drive it on a highway, not just around the block.**
5. **Sleep on it.** Any seller pressuring you to decide today is a reason to walk.
6. **Run the VIN through a vehicle history report** and confirm the seller's name matches the title. No clean title, no sale, no exceptions.

IF IT GOES SIDEWAYS

If you feel yourself getting excited about a specific car, that is the moment to slow down, not speed up. Excitement is what sellers count on.

37 HOW TO UNDERSTAND WHAT INSURANCE ACTUALLY IS

MOVE 01 · GET IT OUT OF YOUR HEAD

THE TEN SECOND VERSION

You pay a small amount regularly so a huge amount is not your problem later.

WHY THIS IS HARDER FOR YOU

Insurance feels like paying for nothing, right up until the day it is the only thing standing between you and a bill you cannot pay.

Understanding three words gets you most of the way there.

DO THIS

1. **Learn premium:** what you pay every month whether anything happens or not.
2. **Learn deductible:** what you pay out of pocket before insurance pays anything.
3. **Learn coverage limit:** the most they will pay. Above that, it is on you.
4. **Know that a lower premium usually means a higher deductible.** You are choosing when to pay, not whether.
5. **Never let car insurance lapse.** Driving uninsured is a legal and financial disaster in every state.

IF IT GOES SIDEWAYS

If the paperwork is overwhelming, call the company and ask them to explain your own policy. They will, and it is their job.

38 HOW TO HANDLE YOUR FIRST PAYCHECK WITHOUT BLOWING IT

MOVE 03 · BUILD IN A DELAY

THE TEN SECOND VERSION

Split it the day it lands. Celebrate with a set amount, not with all of it.

WHY THIS IS HARDER FOR YOU

The first real paycheck feels enormous, and the urge to spend it immediately is genuinely overwhelming. That urge is not a moral failing, it is a reward response doing its job loudly.

Plan the celebration instead of banning it. Banned things get done anyway, just guiltily.

DO THIS

1. **Decide the celebration amount before payday,** maybe twenty percent.
2. **Split the rest the day it lands** using your three account system.
3. **Spend the celebration money on one thing you actually wanted,** not five things you forgot in a week.
4. **Do not upgrade your regular spending** just because income went up
5. **Look at the savings balance at the end of the month.** That number is the reward for the whole system.

IF IT GOES SIDEWAYS

If you already blew it, do not spiral. Start the split on the next check. One check is not a pattern.

39 HOW TO SAY NO TO A PURCHASE YOUR FRIENDS ARE MAKING

MOVE 03 · BUILD IN A DELAY

MOVE 05 · SAY IT EARLY AND SHORT

THE TEN SECOND VERSION

Say you are out this time, with no explanation attached.

WHY THIS IS HARDER FOR YOU

Spending with friends is the hardest spending to control, because you are not just buying a thing, you are buying being included.

Most people respect a clean no far more than they respect a long excuse.

DO THIS

1. **Decide your number before you go out,** not while you are out.
2. **Say I am out this time.** Four words, no story.
3. **Do not explain your finances.** Explanations invite negotiation.
4. **Offer an alternative if you want to stay included.** I will come but I already ate.
5. **Do not lend to cover the gap** so you can join in anyway.

IF IT GOES SIDEWAYS

If someone gives you a hard time about it more than once, that is information about them, not about your budget.

40 HOW TO TRACK SPENDING WITHOUT A COMPLICATED APP

MOVE 06 · BORROW OUTSIDE STRUCTURE

THE TEN SECOND VERSION

Turn on transaction alerts and glance at the total once a week.

WHY THIS IS HARDER FOR YOU

Every budgeting app you have downloaded has been abandoned within eleven days, because they require daily categorizing and daily is not a thing you do reliably.

The best tracking system is the one that runs without your participation.

DO THIS

1. **Turn on a text or push alert for every single transaction.** Awareness in the moment does most of the work.
2. **Use one card for everything** so the record lives in one place.
3. **Look at the week's total every Sunday.** One number, sixty seconds.
4. **Notice the biggest category, not every category.**
5. **Change one thing next week.** One, not the whole life.

IF IT GOES SIDEWAYS

If the alerts get annoying, that annoyance is the feature. Do not turn them off, spend less.

41 HOW TO ORDER FOOD WITHOUT WRECKING A WEEK OF BUDGET

MOVE 04 · CHANGE THE ROOM

THE TEN SECOND VERSION

Delete the apps, keep one meal you can make in ten minutes, and set a delivery limit per week.

WHY THIS IS HARDER FOR YOU

Delivery apps are engineered for impulse, and they charge you three ways: markup, fees, and tip. Twelve dollars of food becomes twenty five without you noticing.

The friction is the whole strategy.

DO THIS

1. **Delete the apps from your phone.** Ordering from a browser is annoying enough to stop half of it.
2. **Pick a weekly limit,** like once, and put it in writing somewhere you see it.
3. **Learn two meals you can make in under ten minutes** and keep those ingredients in the house always.
4. **Eat something small before you order,** because ordering hungry costs more.
5. **Compare the total, not the food price,** when you do order.

IF IT GOES SIDEWAYS

If you order when you are stressed rather than hungry, the fix is not budgeting. Look at what happened that day.

42 HOW TO MOVE OUT WITH MONEY THAT ACTUALLY WORKS

MOVE 01 · GET IT OUT OF YOUR HEAD

THE TEN SECOND VERSION

Add up every monthly cost first. Rent is usually about half of what living costs.

WHY THIS IS HARDER FOR YOU

This one is for later, probably eighteen or after, and it is worth reading now because the mistake gets made in the excited week before anyone does the math. Almost everyone plans for rent and forgets the rest, then discovers that utilities, internet, groceries, laundry, and transportation together cost about as much again.

Do the full math before you sign anything.

DO THIS

1. **Write out every monthly cost:** rent, utilities, internet, phone, food, transportation, insurance.
2. **Add fifteen percent for the things you forgot.** There are always things you forgot.
3. **Compare that total to your actual take home pay,** not your gross.
4. **Save the full move in cost first,** which is usually first month, last month, and a security deposit. On a twelve hundred dollar apartment that is around thirty six hundred dollars before you own a fork.
5. **Set up autopay for rent the day you move in.** Late rent is the most expensive mistake on this list.

IF IT GOES SIDEWAYS

If the numbers do not work, get a roommate before you get a smaller apartment. Splitting fixed costs beats shrinking them.

43 HOW TO NOT GET SCAMMED ONLINE

MOVE 03 · BUILD IN A DELAY

THE TEN SECOND VERSION

Urgency is the tell. Anything rushing you is running a play on you.

WHY THIS IS HARDER FOR YOU

Scams are engineered to work on people who act fast and check later, which is a polite description of exactly how your brain likes to operate. **The good news is that almost every scam uses the same trick:** make you feel like you have to move right now. Once you can see the trick, most of them stop working.

DO THIS

1. **Treat urgency as the alarm bell.** Act now, expires today, your account will be closed. Real organizations are slow and boring and will happily wait for you.
2. **Never click a link in a message about money or an account.** Open the app yourself and look. Takes eleven seconds and defeats most phishing outright.
3. **Never send a gift card to anyone for any reason.** No employer, no government agency, no company on earth needs a gift card. That one is a hundred percent scam, every time.
4. **If a seller wants to move off the platform, that is the scam.** The whole point of the platform is that it protects you.
5. **Say I need to check with someone first** and watch what happens. A real person says sure. A scammer gets aggressive, and now you know.

IF IT GOES SIDEWAYS

If you already sent money, tell an adult today rather than tomorrow. Fast reporting sometimes gets it back, and embarrassment costs more than the money if it stops you from asking.

PART THREE OF FIVE

03 PEOPLE

This is the part most books skip, and it is the part that costs the most. Interrupting, missing a cue, saying the true thing at the wrong moment, going quiet for three weeks and wondering why a friendship faded.

None of that means you are bad with people. It means the timing systems most people run automatically, you have to run on purpose.

Running them on purpose works. It just takes knowing what to run.

44 HOW TO STOP INTERRUPTING WITHOUT LOSING YOUR THOUGHT

MOVE 01 · GET IT OUT OF YOUR HEAD

MOVE 03 · BUILD IN A DELAY

THE TEN SECOND VERSION

Write the first three words down, then wait for the pause.

WHY THIS IS HARDER FOR YOU

You interrupt because you know the thought will vanish if you hold it, and you are right about that. It genuinely will.

So the problem is not impulse control, it is storage. Solve storage and the interrupting stops on its own.

DO THIS

1. **Keep a note open or a scrap of paper nearby** in any conversation that matters.
2. **When a thought arrives, write three words.** Just enough to find it again.
3. **Put your attention back on the person** and actually listen to the rest
4. **Wait for a full stop, not a breath.** A breath is not an invitation.
5. **If you do interrupt, say sorry, go ahead, and mean it.** Then let them finish.

> IF IT GOES SIDEWAYS
>
> *If there is no way to write, squeeze your thumb while holding the thought. A physical anchor buys you about thirty seconds.*

45 HOW TO READ A ROOM WHEN YOU MISSED THE CUE

MOVE 03 · BUILD IN A DELAY

THE TEN SECOND VERSION

Look at three faces. Match your volume and energy to the lowest one.

WHY THIS IS HARDER FOR YOU

You are not missing cues because you do not care. You are usually attending to something else in the room, and the social channel is quiet compared to whatever caught you.

Checking on purpose closes most of the gap.

DO THIS

1. **Pause and look at three people's faces** before you say the next thing.
2. **Check volume first.** If everyone is quieter than you, come down to match.
3. **Check bodies.** Turned toward each other means the conversation is closed for now.
4. **If you cannot tell, ask a question instead of making a statement.** Questions are always safe.
5. **When in doubt, say less and stay.** Staying quiet in a group is not failing at it.

IF IT GOES SIDEWAYS

If you realize you misread it badly, do not narrate the realization. Just adjust and keep going. Most people will not have noticed.

46 HOW TO HANDLE REJECTION SENSITIVITY IN THE MOMENT

MOVE 03 · BUILD IN A DELAY

THE TEN SECOND VERSION

Name it, wait twenty minutes, and do not send anything until then.

WHY THIS IS HARDER FOR YOU

A short text or a flat look can land in your body like a physical hit, way out of proportion to what happened. That reaction is real and it is common with ADHD.

The feeling is not the problem. What you do in the next ten minutes is.

DO THIS

1. **Name it silently:** this is the rejection feeling, and it is bigger than the event.
2. **Do not send, post, or say anything for twenty minutes.** This is the whole skill.
3. **Move your body.** Walk, stairs, cold water on your face.
4. **Ask what else the message could mean.** Busy, tired, texting while driving.
5. **If it still hurts after a day, ask them directly and plainly.** Hey, was something off yesterday.

> IF IT GOES SIDEWAYS
>
> *If this happens constantly and knocks out whole days, it is worth telling a doctor or counselor. It is treatable, and you do not have to just endure it.*

47 HOW TO APOLOGIZE WITHOUT OVER APOLOGIZING

MOVE 05 · SAY IT EARLY AND SHORT

THE TEN SECOND VERSION

Name what you did, say it will not repeat, stop talking.

WHY THIS IS HARDER FOR YOU

Over apologizing turns your mistake into a scene the other person now has to manage, which quietly makes it about you again.

A short apology respects them more than a long one.

DO THIS

1. **Name the specific thing.** I was forty minutes late and did not text.
2. **Do not explain why.** Reasons sound like excuses even when they are true.
3. **Say what you will do differently,** and make it something you can actually do.
4. **Stop talking.** Let them respond however they respond.
5. **Then change the thing.** A repeated apology with no change stops counting.

> IF IT GOES SIDEWAYS
>
> *If they are still upset, do not apologize again in the same conversation. Give it time and let the changed behavior do the work.*

48 HOW TO TEXT WITHOUT SPIRALING OVER A READ RECEIPT

MOVE 03 · BUILD IN A DELAY

THE TEN SECOND VERSION

Assume they are busy. Put the phone face down and do something else.

WHY THIS IS HARDER FOR YOU

A read receipt with no reply is information free space, and your brain will fill it with the worst available story within about ninety seconds.

The story is almost never what happened. People put phones down mid thought constantly.

DO THIS

1. **Set a rule:** no follow up text for at least four hours.
2. **Put the phone face down** and go do something physically elsewhere.
3. **Do not send the double text asking if they are mad.** That question creates the problem it fears.
4. **If it has been a full day, send something normal,** not something about the silence.
5. **Turn off read receipts on your own phone.** On iPhone it is Settings, Apps, Messages, Send Read Receipts. On Android it is inside Messages settings under chat features. It lowers the temperature both directions.

> IF IT GOES SIDEWAYS
>
> *If the waiting is unbearable, that is worth noticing on its own. It usually means something else is going on that day.*

49 HOW TO MAKE A FRIEND WHEN YOU ARE NEW

MOVE 06 · BORROW OUTSIDE STRUCTURE

THE TEN SECOND VERSION

Pick one person, ask one question, and show up again in the same place.

WHY THIS IS HARDER FOR YOU

Friendship is mostly repeated exposure, not charisma. People become friends with whoever is reliably around, which is good news if you are not naturally smooth.

Show up in the same place enough times and it happens on its own.

DO THIS

1. **Pick a place you can return to weekly.** A club, a team, a class, a gym, a job.
2. **Talk to one person, not the group.** Groups are much harder and you do not need them.
3. **Ask about the thing you are both doing.** How long have you been coming to this.
4. **Remember one detail and bring it up next time.** This single move builds more friendship than anything else on this list.
5. **Make one small invitation after three or four weeks of showing up.** Keep it low stakes and specific: a few of us are getting food after, want to come.

> IF IT GOES SIDEWAYS
>
> *If someone does not respond to an invitation twice, move to someone else. It is not a verdict on you, it is a scheduling problem or a fit problem.*

50 HOW TO KEEP A FRIENDSHIP YOU KEEP FORGETTING TO MAINTAIN

MOVE 06 · BORROW OUTSIDE STRUCTURE

MOVE 01 · GET IT OUT OF YOUR HEAD

THE TEN SECOND VERSION

Put the person in your calendar. Reaching out on a schedule still counts.

WHY THIS IS HARDER FOR YOU

Out of sight, out of mind is not a saying for you, it is a description. You can care deeply about someone and not think about them for two months.

Friendships do not usually end in a fight. They end in a slow silence nobody chose.

DO THIS

1. **List the five people you actually want to keep.** Five, not twenty.
2. **Put a repeating reminder in your calendar** for each one, monthly is fine.
3. **When the reminder goes off, send something within sixty seconds.** Do not save it for when you have a better message. The better message never gets sent.
4. **Send the thing that reminded you of them.** A photo, a clip, a memory. It works better than how are you.
5. **Suggest an actual plan every few messages,** because texting alone does not hold a friendship up.

IF IT GOES SIDEWAYS

If you have gone silent for months, do not open with an apology essay. Send something normal. Most people are relieved, not offended.

51 HOW TO DISAGREE WITHOUT IT TURNING INTO A FIGHT

MOVE 03 · BUILD IN A DELAY

MOVE 05 · SAY IT EARLY AND SHORT

THE TEN SECOND VERSION

Agree with the part that is true first, then say your piece once.

WHY THIS IS HARDER FOR YOU

You may go from zero to fully engaged faster than the other person expects, and intensity reads as aggression even when you only meant interest.

Lowering the volume keeps the disagreement about the actual topic.

DO THIS

1. **Find the part they are right about and say it out loud first.** You are right that it cost more.
2. **Use one sentence for your side,** not five.
3. **Talk about the thing, not the person.** That plan has a problem, not you never think.
4. **Ask one real question** and actually wait for the answer.
5. **Let it end unresolved.** Not every disagreement needs a winner today.

> IF IT GOES SIDEWAYS
>
> *If your voice or heart rate is climbing, say I need a minute and step outside. Leaving early beats saying the thing you cannot take back.*

52 HOW TO TAKE CRITICISM WITHOUT SHUTTING DOWN

MOVE 03 · BUILD IN A DELAY

THE TEN SECOND VERSION

Say thanks, ask one clarifying question, and decide tomorrow what to do with it.

WHY THIS IS HARDER FOR YOU

If you have heard corrections your entire life, criticism does not land as information, it lands as evidence in a case that has been running since second grade.

You can separate the two, but not in the first sixty seconds. So do not try to.

DO THIS

1. **Say thanks for telling me,** even while it stings.
2. **Ask one question to make it specific.** Which part specifically.
3. **Do not defend, explain, or list reasons** in that conversation.
4. **Write down what they actually said,** in their words, before your brain edits it into something worse.
5. **Decide tomorrow what is useful in it.** Some of it will be. Not all of it has to be.

IF IT GOES SIDEWAYS

If you feel yourself collapsing into I am terrible at everything, that is the old case running, not this feedback. One comment is about one thing.

53 HOW TO TELL SOMEONE YOU HAVE ADHD

MOVE 05 · SAY IT EARLY AND SHORT

THE TEN SECOND VERSION

Say what it means for them, not the diagnosis history.

WHY THIS IS HARDER FOR YOU

People do not need the clinical explanation, and giving it usually invites a debate about whether ADHD is real, which is not a conversation worth your afternoon.

What helps them is knowing what to expect and what to do.

DO THIS

1. **Pick a calm moment,** not the middle of a problem you just caused.
2. **Keep it to two sentences.** I have ADHD. It mostly means I lose track of time and I need things written down.
3. **Give one specific ask.** If you text me plans, put the time in the text.
4. **Do not apologize for it** or promise it will not affect anything.
5. **Move on to something else.** The shorter you make it, the less of a big deal it becomes.

> IF IT GOES SIDEWAYS
>
> *If someone responds with everyone is a little ADHD, do not argue. Say it is a bit more than that for me, and change the subject.*

54 HOW TO HANDLE BEING LEFT OUT

MOVE 03 · BUILD IN A DELAY

THE TEN SECOND VERSION

Check the facts before the story, then decide if it is worth asking about.

WHY THIS IS HARDER FOR YOU

Seeing a photo you were not in hits harder than it should, and your brain will immediately build a complete narrative about being unwanted.

Most exclusion is logistics, not verdicts. Someone was already there, someone forgot, someone only had one car.

DO THIS

1. **Do not comment on the post.** Anything you write while it stings will read wrong.
2. **Ask what you actually know.** Often it is one photo and nothing else.
3. **Notice if it is a pattern or a single event.** Those need different responses.
4. **If it is a pattern, ask one person directly and calmly.** Hey, am I missing something.
5. **Invite people yourself next time.** The person who plans things is rarely left out.

> IF IT GOES SIDEWAYS
>
> *If you have been left out of the same group repeatedly, put your energy into a different group. That is not giving up, it is spending your time better.*

55 HOW TO STOP TALKING TOO MUCH WHEN YOU ARE EXCITED

MOVE 03 · BUILD IN A DELAY

THE TEN SECOND VERSION

Ask a question every third thing you say.

WHY THIS IS HARDER FOR YOU

When something interests you, the words come fast and the internal monitor that tells most people to wrap up does not fire. You often only notice when someone's face changes.

A simple external rule works better than trying to sense it.

DO THIS

1. **Count.** After three things you say, ask a question.
2. **Watch for the wrap up signals:** shorter answers, phones coming out, feet turning away.
3. **Offer the exit yourself.** Anyway, that is way more than you asked about.
4. **Give the topic to someone who wants it.** A friend who shares the interest is a better audience than a polite stranger.
5. **Save the long version for people who ask for the long version.**

IF IT GOES SIDEWAYS

If you realize you have been going for ten minutes, do not apologize dramatically. Just ask them something and hand the conversation over.

56 HOW TO ASK SOMEONE OUT

MOVE 05 · SAY IT EARLY AND SHORT

THE TEN SECOND VERSION

Be specific, give a day and an activity, and accept the answer either way.

WHY THIS IS HARDER FOR YOU

Vague asks put all the work on the other person and are easy to say no to without meaning to. A specific ask is easier to say yes to and easier to answer honestly.

Specific is also less nerve wracking, because there is only one question.

DO THIS

1. **Ask in person or by call if you can,** and by text if that is genuinely how you talk.
2. **Name a day and an activity.** Do you want to get food Friday after school.
3. **Keep it short.** The whole ask is one or two sentences.
4. **If they say yes, confirm the time and place before the conversation ends.**
5. **If they say no, say all good, and mean it.** Then genuinely drop it.

IF IT GOES SIDEWAYS

If they say maybe or are vague twice, treat it as a no. Chasing an unclear answer costs you more than a clear no would.

57 HOW TO BE A GOOD PARTNER WHEN YOU FORGET THINGS

MOVE 01 · GET IT OUT OF YOUR HEAD

THE TEN SECOND VERSION

Build systems for the things you forget instead of promising to remember.

WHY THIS IS HARDER FOR YOU

Forgetting a plan reads as not caring, no matter how much you actually care, because from the outside they look the same.

Systems are how you make the caring visible.

DO THIS

1. **Put every plan in your calendar while you are still talking about it.** Not later.
2. **Set reminders for birthdays and anniversaries a week ahead,** not the day of.
3. **Say it plainly:** I am going to write this down because I want to actually be there.
4. **When you drop something, own it fast and fix it fast.** Do not go quiet out of shame.
5. **Do one small reliable thing consistently,** like a text every morning. Consistency counts more than grand gestures.

> IF IT GOES SIDEWAYS
>
> *If they say you never listen, they usually mean they do not feel remembered. Ask what would help, then build that into a system.*

58 HOW TO HANDLE A FRIEND WHO ONLY TALKS ABOUT THEMSELVES

MOVE 05 · SAY IT EARLY AND SHORT

THE TEN SECOND VERSION

Decide what the friendship is for, then match your energy to that.

WHY THIS IS HARDER FOR YOU

You may be an unusually good listener, and some people will take as much of that as you offer without ever turning it around.

You are allowed to notice that and adjust how much you give.

DO THIS

1. **Try once directly.** Can I tell you about something going on with me.
2. **Notice what they do with it.** That answer is the real information.
3. **If nothing changes, stop offering the deep stuff** and keep the friendship lighter.
4. **Put your important things where they get received,** with people who ask you questions back.
5. **Do not deliver a speech about it.** Adjust quietly and stay decent.

IF IT GOES SIDEWAYS

If you are drained after every single conversation with someone, that is worth taking seriously even when nothing dramatic is happening.

59 HOW TO SAY NO TO A FRIEND

MOVE 05 · SAY IT EARLY AND SHORT

THE TEN SECOND VERSION

Say no early, keep it short, and do not offer an excuse that can be argued with.

WHY THIS IS HARDER FOR YOU

Excuses invite negotiation. If you say you are tired, they will tell you it will be quick, and now you are in a debate you did not want.

A boundary with no reason attached is harder to argue with than a reason.

DO THIS

1. **Answer as soon as you know,** not the night before.
2. **Say I cannot make it,** full stop.
3. **Skip the reason** unless you actually want to give one.
4. **Offer something else only if you mean it.** Never as a softener.
5. **Do not change your answer if they push.** The first no has to hold or it stops meaning anything.

IF IT GOES SIDEWAYS

If you already said yes and cannot do it, cancel early and clearly. Early cancellation is annoying. Not showing up is a different thing entirely.

60 HOW TO DEAL WITH SOMEONE WHO USES ADHD AGAINST YOU

MOVE 05 · SAY IT EARLY AND SHORT

THE TEN SECOND VERSION

Do not defend the diagnosis. Address the behavior they are actually talking about.

WHY THIS IS HARDER FOR YOU

Some people will use your diagnosis as a weapon in an argument, or as a reason not to take you seriously. Defending ADHD as a concept never wins that exchange.

Pull the conversation back to the specific thing.

DO THIS

1. **Do not argue about whether ADHD is real.** That is a trap and it goes nowhere.
2. **Name the actual issue.** If this is about me being late, let us talk about that.
3. **Own what is yours** without accepting what is not.
4. **Say the line once:** ADHD explains it, it does not excuse it, and I am handling it.
5. **Leave the conversation if it keeps circling back.** Circling is the point for some people.

> IF IT GOES SIDEWAYS
>
> *If it is a teacher, coach, or boss doing this repeatedly, bring in an adult who can advocate for you. That is not tattling, that is how it gets fixed.*

61 HOW TO HAVE A HARD CONVERSATION WITH YOUR PARENTS

MOVE 05 · SAY IT EARLY AND SHORT

THE TEN SECOND VERSION

Ask for a time, lead with what you want, and bring a proposal not a complaint.

WHY THIS IS HARDER FOR YOU

Hard conversations usually happen at the worst moment, in the middle of a conflict, when everyone is already activated. Almost nothing gets decided there.

Choosing the moment is most of the outcome.

DO THIS

1. **Ask for a specific time.** Can we talk after dinner about something.
2. **Lead with what you want, not with the history.** I want to change how curfew works.
3. **Bring an actual proposal,** including what you will do to make it work.
4. **Let them react without matching their volume.**
5. **Ask for a trial period instead of a permanent change.** Can we try it for a month.

> IF IT GOES SIDEWAYS
>
> *If it goes badly, ask to revisit it in a week rather than pushing that night. A week changes more minds than an hour does.*

62 HOW TO RECOGNIZE A FRIENDSHIP THAT IS BAD FOR YOU

MOVE 03 · BUILD IN A DELAY

THE TEN SECOND VERSION

Look at how you feel after, not how fun it is during.

WHY THIS IS HARDER FOR YOU

Some friendships are exciting in the moment and leave you worse every single time, and excitement is very easy for your brain to mistake for connection.

The after feeling is the more honest measure.

DO THIS

1. **Notice how you feel an hour after you leave.** Not during.
2. **Ask if you are more yourself around them or less.**
3. **Count how often you apologize to them** compared to how often they apologize to you.
4. **Check whether they get you into things you regret** and then step back from the consequences.
5. **Reduce contact gradually rather than announcing an ending.** Most friendships end by fading and that is allowed.

> IF IT GOES SIDEWAYS
>
> *If someone gets angry when you spend time with other people, that is not closeness. That is control, and it is worth telling an adult about.*

63 HOW TO BE SOMEONE PEOPLE CAN COUNT ON

MOVE 01 · GET IT OUT OF YOUR HEAD

MOVE 05 · SAY IT EARLY AND SHORT

THE TEN SECOND VERSION

Promise less than you can do, then do it. Every time.

WHY THIS IS HARDER FOR YOU

In the moment, you genuinely mean everything you agree to. The gap opens between meaning it and doing it, and other people only ever see the second part.

Reliability is not a personality trait. It is a set of habits, and habits can be built.

DO THIS

1. **Say yes to less.** Two commitments you keep beats six you meant.
2. **Write down every commitment the moment you make it.** No exceptions for small ones.
3. **Give yourself buffer.** Say Saturday when you could probably do Friday
4. **Communicate before the deadline, not after.** A heads up costs you nothing and buys enormous trust.
5. **Do the small things you said you would do.** Small kept promises build more trust than big ones.

IF IT GOES SIDEWAYS

If you have a history of dropping things, do not announce that you have changed. Just be reliable for three months and let people notice.

64 HOW TO COME BACK AFTER YOU BLEW UP AT YOUR PARENTS

MOVE 03 · BUILD IN A DELAY | MOVE 05 · SAY IT EARLY AND SHORT

THE TEN SECOND VERSION

Wait until you are actually calm, own only your part, and keep it to three sentences.

WHY THIS IS HARDER FOR YOU

The blow up is bad. The forty eight hours of stomping around afterward because you do not know how to walk it back is what actually damages things.

Repair is a skill, and it is not the same as apologizing. Almost nobody teaches it, which is why so many households do the silent thing for three days instead.

DO THIS

1. **Wait until you are genuinely calm,** not fake calm. Fake calm reopens the fight in about ninety seconds.
2. **Go to them.** Whoever crosses the room first ends it, and it might as well be you since you are the one reading a book about this.
3. **Own your part specifically and only your part.** I yelled and slammed the door, that was not okay.
4. **Do not attach a but.** The word but deletes every word in front of it, and everyone in the room knows it.
5. **Say one thing that would help next time,** then go do something normal in the same room. Normal is the actual repair.

IF IT GOES SIDEWAYS

If they are still angry, that is allowed. You do not get to control how fast they come down. Say your piece once and let the next hour do its work.

65 HOW TO LIVE WITH A SIBLING WHO KNOWS EVERY BUTTON

MOVE 03 · BUILD IN A DELAY

THE TEN SECOND VERSION

They are collecting your reaction. Stop paying and the price goes up for them, not you.

WHY THIS IS HARDER FOR YOU

Your sibling has been running experiments on you since you could walk and has excellent data. They know the exact sentence, and they know how long it takes.

The reaction is the whole payment. This is the rare situation where doing nothing is the strong move and not the lazy one.

DO THIS

1. **Name the play in your own head.** This is the thing they do. Naming it takes about eighty percent of the sting out.
2. **Give them the most boring possible response.** Okay. Sure. Hm. Boring is devastating.
3. **Leave the room without a parting line.** The parting line is the payment, delivered late.
4. **Bring the actual issue up later when nobody is winning anything,** if it is a real issue and not just Tuesday.
5. **Ask a parent for a structural fix, not a referee call.** Different rooms for homework beats another lecture about being nice.

IF IT GOES SIDEWAYS

If it has stopped being annoying and started being cruel, or it is physical, that is not sibling stuff anymore. Tell an adult plainly, and keep telling them until something changes.

PART FOUR OF FIVE

04
TAKING CARE OF YOUR BODY AND YOUR HEAD

Nobody warns you that half of what feels like a bad personality is actually a bad night of sleep, an empty stomach, or a body that has not moved in nine hours.

This part is not about becoming a health guy. It is about the small physical stuff that quietly decides how hard everything else in this book is going to be.

Fix the basics and every other skill gets easier. Skip them and none of the others work very well.

THIS BOOK BELONGS TO

FROM

BECAUSE

THIS PAGE IS FOR THE GROWN UP

BEFORE YOU HAND IT OVER

Thank you for buying this. Here is the part that decides whether it works.

> **And if you are the teenager and you read this page anyway:** good. Now you know exactly what I told them. Nothing on this page is behind your back.

Do not present it. A book handed over with a speech about how this could really help you becomes evidence in an old argument before it is ever opened. Leave it on his bed, or in the stack of Christmas things, and say nothing.

Do not ask if he has read it. Not next week, not next month. Asking turns it into an assignment, and he already has enough of those.

Expect it to be used out of order. It is built for that. If he reads eleven pages and uses two of them, the book worked.

If he wants to talk about one, follow his lead. Do not use it as a way into the other nine things you have been meaning to bring up. He will notice, and the book will close.

One last thing. A few pages talk plainly about money, driving, anger, and alcohol. The alcohol page does not assume he is drinking and does not treat it as inevitable. It says the answer is no until he is of legal age, and then it gives him the one thing nobody tells boys with ADHD: that alcohol hits impulse control first, and impulse control is already the system he has the least of to spare. He is going to meet that information eventually. I would rather he met it here, from someone who is not handing him a drink.

66 HOW TO BUILD A HYGIENE ROUTINE THAT ACTUALLY STICKS

MOVE 06 · BORROW OUTSIDE STRUCTURE

MOVE 04 · CHANGE THE ROOM

THE TEN SECOND VERSION

Same order, same place, every day. Keep everything visible.

WHY THIS IS HARDER FOR YOU

Hygiene is a stack of small boring steps with no immediate payoff, which is the exact category your brain skips. It is not about caring how you look.

Make it automatic and the caring becomes unnecessary.

DO THIS

1. **Do the same steps in the same order every day.** Order is what makes it run without thinking.
2. **Keep everything out on the counter,** not in a cabinet. Out of sight really is out of mind.
3. **Attach it to a fixed anchor,** like right after you get out of bed or right before you get in.
4. **Keep backups where you actually need them.** Deodorant in your bag, not only at home.
5. **Put a written list on the mirror for the first two weeks.** Then take it down.

IF IT GOES SIDEWAYS

If showering feels like too many steps on a bad day, do the shortest version. A three minute shower counts.

67 HOW TO FALL ASLEEP WHEN YOUR BRAIN WILL NOT STOP

MOVE 01 · GET IT OUT OF YOUR HEAD

MOVE 04 · CHANGE THE ROOM

THE TEN SECOND VERSION

Get the thoughts out on paper, get off the screen, and keep the wake up time fixed.

WHY THIS IS HARDER FOR YOU

The moment the room goes quiet, your brain finally gets uninterrupted processing time and uses it enthusiastically. That is why bedtime is when everything occurs to you.

Give the thoughts somewhere to go and they stop demanding to be held.

DO THIS

1. **Keep paper by the bed** and dump every thought onto it, unsorted, before lights out.
2. **Stop screens thirty minutes before bed,** or at minimum put the phone across the room.
3. **Keep the room cool and dark,** and use noise if silence makes it worse for you.
4. **Get up at the same time every day,** including weekends. Wake time anchors sleep far better than bedtime does.
5. **If you are still awake after twenty minutes, get up and do something boring** in dim light until you are tired.

IF IT GOES SIDEWAYS

If you have been sleeping badly for weeks and it is affecting your days, mention it to a doctor. Sleep problems and ADHD feed each other, and it is fixable.

68 HOW TO TAKE MEDICATION CONSISTENTLY

MOVE 04 · CHANGE THE ROOM

MOVE 06 · BORROW OUTSIDE STRUCTURE

THE TEN SECOND VERSION

Same time, same place, visible container, one backup dose where you actually are.

WHY THIS IS HARDER FOR YOU

The irony is not lost on anyone: medication that helps with forgetting requires remembering to take it.

The answer is never trying harder to remember. It is putting it somewhere your morning already goes.

DO THIS

1. **Put it where your morning already stops,** next to the toothbrush or the coffee, not in a drawer.
2. **Use a weekly pill organizer** so you can see at a glance whether you took it.
3. **Set a repeating phone alarm for the same time daily** and label it with the actual medication name, not just meds. A labeled alarm gets dismissed less.
4. **Keep a backup dose in your bag** for the days you leave in a hurry.
5. **Never adjust the dose yourself.** Tell the prescriber what is happening and let them change it.

IF IT GOES SIDEWAYS

If it makes you feel bad, or wears off too early, or stops working, that is a conversation with the prescriber, not a reason to quit quietly.

69 HOW TO EAT WHEN COOKING FEELS IMPOSSIBLE

MOVE 04 · CHANGE THE ROOM

THE TEN SECOND VERSION

Keep five no cook foods in the house and eat something before you get to empty.

WHY THIS IS HARDER FOR YOU

You forget to eat until you are suddenly furious and cannot think, and by then cooking anything is out of the question. That crash makes everything else harder for hours.

Low effort food that exists beats good food that requires a plan.

DO THIS

1. **Keep five foods in the house that need zero cooking.** Fruit, yogurt, nuts, bread, cheese, deli meat.
2. **Eat within an hour of waking up,** even something small.
3. **Set a lunch alarm** if your day does not have a built in break.
4. **Keep something in your bag** for the days a meal gets skipped anywa
5. **Keep a water bottle with you and refill it three times a day.** A large share of afternoon fog is dehydration, not tiredness.

IF IT GOES SIDEWAYS

If medication kills your appetite completely, eat a real breakfast before it kicks in and a real dinner after it wears off. Tell your prescriber too.

70 HOW TO LEARN FIVE MEALS YOU CAN MAKE

MOVE 02 · SHRINK THE FIRST STEP

THE TEN SECOND VERSION

Pick five, make each three times, and keep the ingredients permanently stocked.

WHY THIS IS HARDER FOR YOU

Recipes are long lists of steps with a hard fail state, which is not a friendly format for you. But five meals you know by heart is enough to feed yourself forever.

Depth beats variety here. Five is genuinely enough.

DO THIS

1. **Pick five meals with six ingredients or fewer.** Eggs, pasta, rice bowls, sandwiches, sheet pan chicken.
2. **Make one of them three times in a row.** Repetition is what turns a recipe into a skill.
3. **Keep every ingredient for those five permanently on the shopping list.**
4. **Prep while something else cooks,** so the timing stops feeling chaotic.
5. **Clean as you go.** The pile at the end is what stops people from cooking again.

> IF IT GOES SIDEWAYS
>
> *If you burn something, that is normal and not a sign you cannot cook. Turn the heat down one notch and try the same thing again.*

71 HOW TO GET OFF YOUR PHONE AT NIGHT

MOVE 04 · CHANGE THE ROOM

THE TEN SECOND VERSION

Charge it in another room, put the screen on a grayscale schedule, and use a real alarm clock.

WHY THIS IS HARDER FOR YOU

Apps are engineered by very smart people to defeat exactly the kind of self control you are trying to use, and they are better at their job than you are at resisting.

Distance works. Discipline does not.

DO THIS

1. **Buy a five dollar alarm clock** so the phone has no reason to be in the room at all.
2. **Charge the phone in another room starting tonight,** not next week.
3. **Put the screen on grayscale automatically at night.** On iPhone, open Shortcuts, tap Automation, choose Time of Day, and add the Set Color Filters action. On Android, turn on Bedtime mode in Digital Wellbeing, which includes grayscale.
4. **Set a daily time limit on the one app you lose the most time to.** Screen Time on iPhone, Digital Wellbeing on Android. One app, not five.
5. **Put a book or headphones on the nightstand** so your hands have a replacement. Audio holds you without a screen keeping you up.

> IF IT GOES SIDEWAYS
>
> *If you tap through the time limit every night, have a parent or a friend set the passcode. Not knowing the code is the part that makes it work.*

72 HOW TO MOVE YOUR BODY WHEN THE GYM IS OVERWHELMING

MOVE 02 · SHRINK THE FIRST STEP

MOVE 06 · BORROW OUTSIDE STRUCTURE

THE TEN SECOND VERSION

Ten minutes of anything, at the same time each day, with no gym involved.

WHY THIS IS HARDER FOR YOU

Exercise genuinely helps ADHD symptoms, which is annoying because starting an exercise routine requires the exact skills ADHD makes hard.

The gym is not the requirement. Movement is.

DO THIS

1. **Pick something with zero setup.** Walking, running, biking, jumping rope, basketball.
2. **Start with ten minutes.** Not forty five, not five days a week.
3. **Do it at the same time every day,** so it stops being a decision.
4. **Pair it with something you like,** a podcast, a playlist, a friend.
5. **Do not track anything for the first month.** Tracking becomes a reason to quit when the numbers dip.

> IF IT GOES SIDEWAYS
>
> *If you miss a week, restart at ten minutes rather than trying to make up for it. Making up for it is how people quit.*

73 HOW TO HANDLE BEING OVERSTIMULATED

MOVE 03 · BUILD IN A DELAY

THE TEN SECOND VERSION

Leave the room, reduce input, and give it ten minutes before deciding anything.

WHY THIS IS HARDER FOR YOU

Too much noise, light, and movement at once does not just annoy you, it uses up the resources you need for patience and judgment. That is when you snap at someone who did nothing.

Leaving is not rude. Staying and blowing up is worse for everyone.

DO THIS

1. **Recognize the early signs.** Jaw tight, irritable, sounds getting sharpe
2. **Leave the room.** Bathroom, hallway, outside, car. Anywhere with less.
3. **Cut input.** Headphones on with nothing playing, or eyes closed, or dim light.
4. **Give it ten minutes** before you decide anything or say anything.
5. **Have a line ready for later.** I needed a minute, I am good now.

IF IT GOES SIDEWAYS

If certain places always do this to you, plan for them in advance. Earplugs in a pocket are a legitimate strategy, not a weakness.

74 HOW TO MANAGE A DAY WITH NO MOTIVATION

MOVE 02 · SHRINK THE FIRST STEP

THE TEN SECOND VERSION

Lower the bar to one thing, do it badly, and let the day be small.

WHY THIS IS HARDER FOR YOU

Some days the fuel is just not there, and no amount of yelling at yourself produces it. Fighting the day usually costs more than the day was worth.

A small completed day beats a big failed one.

DO THIS

1. **Pick one thing that has to happen today.** One.
2. **Do the worst acceptable version of it.** Done badly still counts as done.
3. **Handle the physical basics.** Eat, water, get outside for five minutes.
4. **Do not open the full to do list.** On a low day it just proves a point you do not need proven.
5. **Go to bed at a normal time** so tomorrow starts from a better place.

IF IT GOES SIDEWAYS

If low days start stacking up into weeks, or you stop caring about things you normally like, tell someone. That is a different thing and it is worth getting help for.

75 HOW TO NOTICE WHAT YOUR BODY IS TELLING YOU

MOVE 03 · BUILD IN A DELAY

THE TEN SECOND VERSION

Check hunger, sleep, and movement before you believe your mood.

WHY THIS IS HARDER FOR YOU

You are more likely than most people to miss internal signals until they are shouting, which means hunger arrives as rage and tiredness arrives as hopelessness.

Check the body first. A surprising amount of the mood turns out to be logistics.

DO THIS

1. **When you feel awful, run the checklist:** when did I last eat, how did I sleep, have I moved.
2. **Fix whatever is missing before you analyze the feeling.**
3. **Wait thirty minutes after fixing it** and check the mood again.
4. **If it is genuinely gone, note what caused it** so you catch it faster next time.
5. **If it is still there, then treat it as real** and deal with the actual thing

IF IT GOES SIDEWAYS

This does not mean feelings are never real. It means running the physical checklist first saves you from a lot of unnecessary spirals.

76 HOW TO USE MUSIC AND NOISE ON PURPOSE

MOVE 04 · CHANGE THE ROOM

THE TEN SECOND VERSION

Instrumental for focus, familiar for boring tasks, silence when you are already overloaded.

WHY THIS IS HARDER FOR YOU

Total silence is often worse for you than sound, because your brain will manufacture stimulation if none is provided. But the wrong sound eats the attention you were trying to protect.

Different tasks want different noise.

DO THIS

1. **Use instrumental or lyric free music for reading and writing.** Lyrics compete for the language part of your brain.
2. **Use familiar music you have heard a thousand times for boring tasks,** because it does not pull attention.
3. **Try brown noise, a fan, or rain sounds** when music is too much but silence is worse. Brown noise is on every streaming app and on YouTube for free.
4. **Build two playlists and stop choosing every time.** Choosing is its own distraction.
5. **Go silent when you are already overstimulated.** Sound is not always the answer.

IF IT GOES SIDEWAYS

If you spend fifteen minutes picking music before every study session, that is procrastination in a costume. Pick a default and start.

77 HOW TO GO TO A DOCTOR APPOINTMENT AND ACTUALLY GET WHAT YOU NEED

MOVE 01 · GET IT OUT OF YOUR HEAD

THE TEN SECOND VERSION

Write your three questions down beforehand and take notes during.

WHY THIS IS HARDER FOR YOU

Appointments are short, you are nervous, and you will remember the important question in the parking lot afterward. That is not a personal failing, that is how appointments work.

Paper solves it.

DO THIS

1. **Write down your top three questions before you go** and put them in order of importance.
2. **Write down what has actually been happening,** with rough dates. Memory is unreliable under pressure.
3. **Ask the most important question first,** not last.
4. **Take notes during the appointment** or ask if you can record it.
5. **Repeat the plan back before you leave.** So I am doing this, and coming back in six weeks.

IF IT GOES SIDEWAYS

If you do not understand something, say I did not follow that, can you say it another way. Every good doctor would rather explain twice than have you leave confused.

78 HOW TO HANDLE A HYPERFOCUS SESSION WITHOUT WRECKING YOUR DAY

MOVE 06 · BORROW OUTSIDE STRUCTURE

MOVE 04 · CHANGE THE ROOM

THE TEN SECOND VERSION

Set alarms before you start, and put water and food within reach.

WHY THIS IS HARDER FOR YOU

Hyperfocus is the best thing your brain does and the least controllable. Six hours vanish, you have built something remarkable, and you have not eaten or moved or answered anyone.

You do not want to stop it. You want to fence it.

DO THIS

1. **Set an alarm before you start,** not once you are in. Once you are in, you will not set it.
2. **Put water and something to eat within arm's reach** before you begin.
3. **Tell someone what you are doing** if you have somewhere to be later.
4. **Use a second alarm across the room** for the hard deadline, so you have to stand up.
5. **Write one sentence about where you stopped and what comes next** before you close everything. Re entry tomorrow takes two minutes instead of twenty.

> IF IT GOES SIDEWAYS
>
> *If you blow through the alarms regularly, put the thing you have to leave for in the calendar with a fifteen minute and a five minute warning.*

79 HOW TO TAKE A REAL BREAK

MOVE 04 · CHANGE THE ROOM

THE TEN SECOND VERSION

Get up, move, and stay off the screen. Set a timer for the break too.

WHY THIS IS HARDER FOR YOU

Scrolling is not a break. It gives your brain the same kind of input it just had, so you come back more tired and no more ready to work.

A real break changes the channel.

DO THIS

1. **Stand up and leave the room.** The break starts when your body moves.
2. **Do something physical,** stairs, stretching, walking outside, getting water.
3. **Set a timer for the break itself,** ten minutes, or the break eats the afternoon.
4. **Keep the phone out of it** if you want the break to actually restore anything.
5. **Come back to a task you already started,** not a new one. Restarting is easier than starting.

IF IT GOES SIDEWAYS

If breaks always turn into an hour, take your break somewhere without a comfortable place to sit.

80 HOW TO DEAL WITH A RACING MIND DURING THE DAY

MOVE 01 · GET IT OUT OF YOUR HEAD

THE TEN SECOND VERSION

Dump everything onto paper, circle one thing, and do it.

WHY THIS IS HARDER FOR YOU

When twelve things are all live at once, none of them get worked on, and the noise itself becomes exhausting. That is not anxiety necessarily, it is unsorted load.

Getting it out of your head shrinks it every time.

DO THIS

1. **Write every open thing down,** in any order, without sorting.
2. **Look at the list.** It is usually shorter than the noise suggested.
3. **Cross off anything that is not actually yours to handle.**
4. **Circle one thing and do only that.**
5. **Leave the list where you can see it** so your brain stops rehearsing it to keep it alive.

IF IT GOES SIDEWAYS

If the racing does not stop after the list, go move for ten minutes. Physical activity clears it faster than thinking about it does.

81 HOW TO TAKE CARE OF YOUR TEETH WHEN IT FEELS POINTLESS

MOVE 04 · CHANGE THE ROOM

MOVE 06 · BORROW OUTSIDE STRUCTURE

THE TEN SECOND VERSION

Keep a brush where you already are, and brush for a song.

WHY THIS IS HARDER FOR YOU

Dental work is expensive, painful, and entirely preventable, and none of that motivates you at eleven at night when you are already in bed.

So do not rely on motivation. Reduce the distance to the toothbrush.

DO THIS

1. **Keep a toothbrush wherever you actually end up,** including a second one if you never make it back to the bathroom.
2. **Brush at the same anchor point every day,** like right after you eat breakfast.
3. **Play one song and brush for the song.** Time blindness makes two minutes impossible to feel.
4. **Keep floss picks visible** instead of floss in a drawer.
5. **Go to a dentist twice a year,** and put both appointments in the calendar at once.

IF IT GOES SIDEWAYS

If you have skipped for a long time and are dreading the appointment, tell them that when you book. They deal with it constantly and they will not lecture you.

82 HOW TO HANDLE ALCOHOL AND ANYTHING ELSE THAT CHANGES HOW YOU FEEL

MOVE 03 · BUILD IN A DELAY

THE TEN SECOND VERSION

Right now the answer is no. Later, know this: all of it goes after impulse control first, and yours is already stretched thin.

WHY THIS IS HARDER FOR YOU

You are not old enough for any of this yet, and that is the law plus a brain still finishing construction. But you will be one day, sooner than it feels, and nobody hands this out at the door.

Alcohol, nicotine, and cannabis all work on the systems your ADHD already taxes, and **they go after impulse control before anything else.** The gap between one and too many is smaller for you than for your friends, and it closes faster.

DO THIS

1. **Until you are of legal age the answer is no, and you owe nobody a reason.** I am good is a complete sentence and beats a story that can be argued with.
2. **Know that ADHD carries a higher than average risk of substance problems.** Not a certainty. A higher risk, which you want to know in advance rather than discover.
3. **Understand vapes specifically.** Nicotine sharpens focus for a few minutes, which makes it feel like it is helping, and that is exactly why it hooks ADHD brains harder and faster.
4. **Know that regular cannabis use in the teenage years is linked to attention and memory problems.** That is the last place you need a second hit.
5. **Assume anything you take interacts with your medication** until a prescriber says otherwise. Ask before, not after.
6. **Decide your limits while you are sober and at home,** not in a room with people handing you things.
7. **Settle your ride home before you leave the house.** Every time, for the rest of your life.

IF IT GOES SIDEWAYS

If you cannot stick to a limit you set, or you are using something to focus, sleep, or take the edge off, tell a doctor or an adult you trust. Getting ahead of it is far easier than catching up to it.

83 HOW TO GET YOURSELF OUTSIDE EVERY DAY

MOVE 06 · BORROW OUTSIDE STRUCTURE

THE TEN SECOND VERSION

Attach it to something you already do, and keep it to ten minutes.

WHY THIS IS HARDER FOR YOU

Morning light helps set your sleep clock, which is often shifted late with ADHD, and being outdoors reliably lifts mood in a way that does not require you to believe in it.

It is one of the cheapest interventions available.

DO THIS

1. **Go out within an hour of waking** if you can, even for five minutes.
2. **Attach it to something existing.** Walk to get coffee, walk the dog, take the trash out slowly.
3. **Do not check your phone while you are out there.**
4. **Keep shoes and a jacket by the door** so friction does not stop you.
5. **Go even when the weather is bad.** Ten bad minutes still counts.

IF IT GOES SIDEWAYS

If ten minutes feels like too much, stand in the doorway for two. Light is doing most of the work anyway.

84 HOW TO KNOW WHEN SOMETHING BIGGER IS GOING ON

MOVE 05 · SAY IT EARLY AND SHORT

THE TEN SECOND VERSION

Watch for changes that last weeks, not days, and tell someone.

WHY THIS IS HARDER FOR YOU

ADHD often travels with other things, and it can be hard to tell what is a hard week and what is something that needs actual help.

The distinguishing feature is usually duration and reach. A bad few days is normal. A changed few weeks is worth checking.

DO THIS

1. **Notice how long it has been going on.** Days are normal. Weeks are worth attention.
2. **Notice whether it is touching everything,** sleep, school, friends, food, interest in things you like.
3. **Say it to one adult you trust, plainly.** Use the actual words: I have not felt right for about three weeks and I want to see somebody.
4. **Ask for a doctor appointment.** You are allowed to ask for this directly
5. **Do not wait for it to get worse to qualify.** Earlier is easier, always.

IF IT GOES SIDEWAYS

If you do not know who to tell, tell a school counselor. That is literally what they are there for, and it does not have to become a big thing.

85 HOW TO BE DECENT TO YOURSELF ABOUT ALL OF THIS

MOVE 03 · BUILD IN A DELAY

THE TEN SECOND VERSION

Talk to yourself the way you would talk to a friend with the same problem.

WHY THIS IS HARDER FOR YOU

You have probably heard corrections since you were small, and that voice tends to move inside and keep going on its own. It sounds like honesty. It is not, it is just a habit.

Nobody has ever improved because someone yelled at them for years, including when the someone was themselves.

DO THIS

1. **Notice the voice when it starts.** Naming it takes most of its power.
2. **Ask what you would say to a friend** who just did the same thing.
3. **Say that version instead,** out loud if you can.
4. **Separate the mistake from the identity.** I forgot, not I am the guy who forgets everything.
5. **Notice one thing that went right today,** even a small one. Your brain does not log those automatically.

> IF IT GOES SIDEWAYS
>
> *If the voice is constant and cruel and does not let up, that is worth telling a counselor about. It is a common thing to carry and it does get better with help.*

86 HOW TO CATCH ANGER BEFORE IT RUNS THE ROOM

MOVE 03 · BUILD IN A DELAY

THE TEN SECOND VERSION

Your body knows first. Leave at the warm stage, not the hot one.

WHY THIS IS HARDER FOR YOU

You probably do not go from calm to furious. It just feels that way, because the first four steps happen somewhere below the level you notice, and then you are already talking.

You cannot stop anger at the top. Nobody can. You can only catch it early, which means learning what early feels like in your specific body.

DO THIS

1. **Learn your two earliest signs.** Usually jaw, chest, hands, ears getting hot, or talking faster. Two is enough.
2. **Leave at the first one.** I need a minute is a complete sentence and it works on parents, teachers, coaches, and bosses.
3. **Move hard for ninety seconds.** Stairs, push ups, a fast walk. Anger is physical fuel and it burns off faster if you spend it.
4. **Do not rehearse the argument while you are gone.** Rehearsing is how you come back angrier than you left.
5. **Come back and say the one thing you actually meant,** in a normal voice. This is the part that changes how people see you.

IF IT GOES SIDEWAYS

If you keep blowing past the early signs, ask someone who is around you a lot what they see first. They will know immediately, because they have been watching for it for years.

87 HOW TO STOP COMPARING YOURSELF TO EVERYONE ON YOUR PHONE

MOVE 04 · CHANGE THE ROOM

THE TEN SECOND VERSION

You are comparing your whole life to their highlight reel. Mute the accounts that do it to you.

WHY THIS IS HARDER FOR YOU

Nobody posts the boring part, the failed part, or the eleventh take. You are measuring your unedited Tuesday against three hundred people's best week, and then wondering why you come up short.

The math is rigged and it is rigged on purpose, because feeling slightly behind is what keeps you scrolling.

DO THIS

1. **Notice which accounts leave you worse.** Not which ones are bad. Which ones make you feel like garbage specifically.
2. **Mute or unfollow them.** Mute is invisible, so nobody has their feelings hurt and you get your afternoon back.
3. **Fill the gap with something,** or the feed just recommends you five more. Follow people who make things instead of people who show things.
4. **Set one no phone block a day,** even thirty minutes. The comparison stops the moment the source does.
5. **When it hits anyway, say the true sentence:** I am comparing my whole self to one photo somebody chose.

IF IT GOES SIDEWAYS

If a whole platform makes you feel worse every time and you keep opening it anyway, delete the app for two weeks. Not forever. Two weeks tells you a lot.

88 HOW TO HANDLE BEING BORED WITHOUT WRECKING SOMETHING

MOVE 03 · BUILD IN A DELAY	MOVE 04 · CHANGE THE ROOM

THE TEN SECOND VERSION

Have three things ready before boredom hits. Boredom is not a mood, it is a hunger.

WHY THIS IS HARDER FOR YOU

Boredom is genuinely more painful for you than for other people, and that is not you being dramatic. An understimulated brain will manufacture stimulation using whatever is available, which is how arguments start and dumb decisions get made at eleven at night.

Boredom is the setup for most of the trouble you get into. Not the trouble itself. The setup.

DO THIS

1. **Write three things you can start in under a minute** and keep the list on your phone. Instrument, sketchbook, run, game, book, whatever.
2. **Notice the feeling and name it.** I am bored, not I am restless and everyone is annoying, which is what it disguises itself as.
3. **Pick one and start it badly.** Waiting to feel like it is how the whole evening goes sideways.
4. **Get moving if none of them work.** Physical beats digital here almost every time, and you already know that.
5. **Do not text the person you should not text.** That is boredom driving, and boredom is a terrible driver.

> IF IT GOES SIDEWAYS
>
> *If boredom regularly turns into risky decisions, build more into your week on purpose. A team, a job, a band. Structure beats self control every time.*

PART FIVE OF FIVE

05
HANDLING WHAT COMES NEXT

At some point the adults who have been managing your accommodations, your appointments, and your deadlines are going to stop, and the handoff usually happens faster than anyone plans for.

The good news is that self advocacy is a skill, not a personality. It is a set of sentences you can learn and a set of moves you can practice before you need them.

This part is about being the person who runs your own situation. Not perfectly. Just yourself.

89 HOW TO ASK A TEACHER FOR WHAT YOU NEED

MOVE 05 · SAY IT EARLY AND SHORT

THE TEN SECOND VERSION

Go before class, name one specific thing, and say what you will do in return.

WHY THIS IS HARDER FOR YOU

Most teachers will help. What stops them is a vague request in the hallway thirty seconds before the bell, which they cannot act on even if they want to.

Specific and early is the whole difference.

DO THIS

1. **Go before or after class, never during.** Email works too if you are nervous.
2. **Ask for one thing, specifically.** Can I get the slides ahead of time, or can I sit closer to the front.
3. **Explain what it does for you in one sentence,** not a medical history
4. **Say what you will do on your end.** I will still turn everything in on time.
5. **Thank them and then actually follow through.** Following through is what makes the next ask easy.

> IF IT GOES SIDEWAYS
>
> *If a teacher says no, do not argue. Ask what would work instead, or go to your counselor. There is usually another route.*

90 HOW TO UNDERSTAND YOUR OWN ACCOMMODATIONS

MOVE 01 · GET IT OUT OF YOUR HEAD

THE TEN SECOND VERSION

Read your own plan, know what it says, and be able to name what you use.

WHY THIS IS HARDER FOR YOU

Plenty of students have accommodations they have never read, which means they cannot ask for them, cannot explain them, and lose them the moment the adult who set them up is gone.

Knowing what is on your own paperwork is basic self defense.

DO THIS

1. **Ask your counselor to show you your own IEP or 504 plan.** You have the right to read it, and asking in an email gets a faster response than asking in a hallway.
2. **Write down the three accommodations you actually use.**
3. **Learn to say each one in a sentence.** I get extended time on tests.
4. **Ask to be in the meeting about it,** and say what is and is not working.
5. **Ask what happens to it after high school,** because the system changes completely at college and at work.

IF IT GOES SIDEWAYS

If nobody will show you the plan, ask your counselor directly and in writing. A written request tends to move faster than a spoken one.

91 HOW TO STUDY FOR A TEST WHEN REVIEWING IS BORING

MOVE 02 · SHRINK THE FIRST STEP

THE TEN SECOND VERSION

Test yourself instead of rereading. Short sessions, spread out.

WHY THIS IS HARDER FOR YOU

Rereading notes feels like studying and is close to useless for anyone, and for you it is worse, because passive material cannot hold your attention long enough to encode.

Retrieval is what builds memory. Making yourself answer beats looking at answers.

DO THIS

1. **Turn your notes into questions,** then answer them from memory.
2. **Study in twenty five minute blocks with five minute breaks.**
3. **Spread it over at least three days.** Three twenty five minute sessions on three days beat one three hour night, by a wide margin.
4. **Say the answers out loud or teach them to someone,** even an empty room.
5. **Spend your time on what you got wrong,** not on rereading what you already know.

IF IT GOES SIDEWAYS

If you cannot make yourself start, do one question. One question is a small enough ask to get past the wall.

92 HOW TO PASS THE WRITTEN DRIVING TEST

MOVE 02 · SHRINK THE FIRST STEP

THE TEN SECOND VERSION

Take practice tests until you score high twice in a row, then take the real one.

WHY THIS IS HARDER FOR YOU

The handbook is long and dry, and reading it front to back is the least effective study method available to you.

Practice tests are the actual study method. They are retrieval, they are short, and they show you exactly what you do not know.

DO THIS

1. **Skip reading the handbook cover to cover.** Use it as a reference instead.
2. **Take a free practice test immediately, before studying anything.** Your state DMV website has official ones, and the handbook is a free PDF on the same site.
3. **Look up only the questions you missed** in the handbook.
4. **Repeat until you score above ninety percent twice in a row** on tests you have not seen before.
5. **Book the real test right after that second good score,** while it is fresh.

> IF IT GOES SIDEWAYS
>
> *If you fail, you can retake it. Almost everyone who fails passes the second time, and nobody ever asks how many tries it took.*

93 HOW TO DRIVE SAFELY WITH AN ADHD BRAIN

MOVE 04 · CHANGE THE ROOM

THE TEN SECOND VERSION

Phone out of reach before you start. No passengers while you are new.

WHY THIS IS HARDER FOR YOU

Driving is a sustained attention task with life or death consequences, and distraction risk is genuinely higher with ADHD. That is not a reason not to drive, it is a reason to set rules.

Set the rules while the car is parked.

DO THIS

1. **Put the phone in the glove box or the back seat** before you start the engine. Not on the seat.
2. **Set the music and the navigation before you move,** not at a red light.
3. **Drive alone while you are new.** Passengers are the biggest distraction there is for young drivers.
4. **Leave earlier than you need to.** Rushing is where the bad decisions live.
5. **Pull over if you are upset.** Driving angry is genuinely dangerous and very common.

IF IT GOES SIDEWAYS

If you notice yourself arriving somewhere with no memory of the drive, that is a sign to cut the distractions further and get more sleep.

94 HOW TO RECOVER FROM FAILING SOMETHING

MOVE 03 · BUILD IN A DELAY

THE TEN SECOND VERSION

Feel it for a day, find the one fixable cause, and take one action.

WHY THIS IS HARDER FOR YOU

Failure tends to land as confirmation rather than information, because you have a long file of similar moments and your brain will happily open all of it.

One failure is one event. It is not a summary of you, even though it feels like one.

DO THIS

1. **Give yourself a day to feel bad about it.** Do not skip this and do not extend it.
2. **Write what actually happened,** in facts, without adjectives.
3. **Find the one thing you could change.** Usually it is starting earlier, not trying harder.
4. **Take one action within forty eight hours.** Email the teacher, ask about a retake, sign up again.
5. **Tell one person.** Carrying it alone is what turns an event into a story about yourself.

> IF IT GOES SIDEWAYS
>
> *If you cannot stop replaying it after a couple of weeks, talk to someone. Replaying is a loop, and loops do not resolve on their own.*

95 HOW TO SET A GOAL YOU WILL STILL CARE ABOUT IN THREE WEEKS

MOVE 02 · SHRINK THE FIRST STEP

MOVE 04 · CHANGE THE ROOM

THE TEN SECOND VERSION

Make it small, make it visible, and attach the first step to a date.

WHY THIS IS HARDER FOR YOU

Your goals fail at week three because the newness wears off and nothing else was holding them up. Interest was doing all the work.

Build something that works after the interest fades, because it will.

DO THIS

1. **Make the goal smaller than feels impressive.** Impressive goals are for the version of you who is excited today.
2. **Write the first step as a specific action with a date,** not as an intention.
3. **Put it somewhere you physically see it every day.**
4. **Track it in the crudest possible way,** an X on a calendar. Complicated tracking gets abandoned.
5. **Plan for week three now.** Decide today what you will do when you stop caring.

IF IT GOES SIDEWAYS

If you have abandoned it, restart at half the size instead of giving up on the goal. The size was wrong, not the goal.

96 HOW TO DECIDE WHAT TO DO AFTER HIGH SCHOOL

MOVE 02 · SHRINK THE FIRST STEP

THE TEN SECOND VERSION

Test things cheaply before committing. Try before you decide.

WHY THIS IS HARDER FOR YOU

You are being asked to pick a direction with almost no real information, and the pressure to sound certain makes people commit to things they have never actually tried.

Trying is much cheaper than committing. Do the cheap thing first.

DO THIS

1. **List what you actually like doing,** not what sounds impressive.
2. **Find the cheapest way to test each one.** A summer job, a shadow day, a short course, a conversation.
3. **Talk to three people who do the thing** and ask what the bad days look like.
4. **Look at trades and certificates as seriously as four year college.** They are faster, cheaper, and often a better fit.
5. **Pick a direction, not a destination.** You are allowed to change it, and most people do.

IF IT GOES SIDEWAYS

If everyone around you assumes one path, you are still allowed to look at others. Their certainty is not information about you.

97 HOW TO GET ACCOMMODATIONS IN COLLEGE

MOVE 05 · SAY IT EARLY AND SHORT

MOVE 01 · GET IT OUT OF YOUR HEAD

THE TEN SECOND VERSION

Nobody comes to find you. You register with the disability office yourself.

WHY THIS IS HARDER FOR YOU

This is the single biggest surprise in the transition. High school finds you and builds a plan. College does not, legally cannot, and will not know you exist unless you tell them.

Every year, students lose accommodations they qualified for simply because nobody told them this.

DO THIS

1. **Find the disability or accessibility services office** during your first week, before classes get hard.
2. **Bring documentation of your diagnosis.** Most schools want a recent evaluation report from a doctor or psychologist. An IEP or 504 plan alone is often not enough, so request the full evaluation from your school before you graduate.
3. **Register even if you think you will not need it.** Registering early and not using it beats scrambling in November.
4. **Learn how to renew each semester,** because most schools require you to request your accommodation letters again every term. Put it in your calendar for the first week of every semester.
5. **Email your professors yourself in week one.** The office approves it, but you deliver it.

IF IT GOES SIDEWAYS

If you do not have documentation, ask the office what they will accept. Requirements vary and many schools are more flexible than you expect.

98 HOW TO MANAGE YOURSELF WITH NO ONE CHECKING ON YOU

MOVE 06 · BORROW OUTSIDE STRUCTURE

THE TEN SECOND VERSION

Build external structure on purpose, because nobody is going to provide it anymore.

WHY THIS IS HARDER FOR YOU

High school is a structure machine. Bells, attendance, teachers noticing. When it goes away, a lot of people who were doing fine fall apart within a semester.

The structure was doing more work than you realized. You have to rebuild it yourself.

DO THIS

1. **Put everything in a calendar,** including things that are not appointments, like study blocks and meals.
2. **Go to the same place at the same time to work.** Location is a powerful cue.
3. **Find one recurring commitment with other people,** a job, a team, a club. It anchors the week.
4. **Check in with someone weekly,** a friend, a parent, an advisor.
5. **Notice a slide in week two, not week eight.** Missing two classes is fixable. Missing three weeks is a different problem.

> IF IT GOES SIDEWAYS
>
> *If you are already behind, go to the professor or the advisor immediately. Almost every recoverable situation gets unrecoverable through silence.*

99 HOW TO WRITE AN EMAIL AN ADULT WILL TAKE SERIOUSLY

MOVE 05 · SAY IT EARLY AND SHORT

THE TEN SECOND VERSION

Clear subject, three sentences, specific ask, your name.

WHY THIS IS HARDER FOR YOU

A long unclear email gets moved to later and later never arrives. A short clear one gets answered the same day.

You are not writing an essay. You are making a request easy to say yes to.

DO THIS

1. **Write a subject line that says the thing.** Question about Friday's exam, not hello.
2. **Open with who you are and which class or context.**
3. **Put the ask in the second sentence,** and make it specific.
4. **Keep the whole thing under five sentences.**
5. **Sign it with your full name,** and send it from an address that is your actual name.

> IF IT GOES SIDEWAYS
>
> *If you get no reply after five business days, send one short follow up. One. Then find another way to ask.*

FULL EXAMPLE ON PAGE 130

100 HOW TO ADVOCATE FOR YOURSELF AT WORK

MOVE 05 · SAY IT EARLY AND SHORT

THE TEN SECOND VERSION

Ask for the tool, not the exception. Frame it as what makes you better at the job.

WHY THIS IS HARDER FOR YOU

You do not have to disclose a diagnosis to ask for something that helps you work. Most of what you need sounds completely normal when you ask for it directly.

Written instructions are a reasonable request for anyone.

DO THIS

1. **Ask for the specific tool.** Can you send that by text so I have it in writing.
2. **Frame it around the work,** not around you. It helps me get the order right.
3. **Ask early, in a calm moment,** not after a mistake.
4. **Write things down visibly during instructions.** Managers read that as competence.
5. **Only disclose a diagnosis if you want formal accommodations,** which are protected under the Americans with Disabilities Act. Ask HR what their process is before you disclose anything.

IF IT GOES SIDEWAYS

If a manager refuses reasonable requests and the job is making you worse, that is information about the job. Some environments fit better than others.

101 HOW TO HANDLE A DEADLINE YOU ARE GOING TO MISS

MOVE 05 · SAY IT EARLY AND SHORT

THE TEN SECOND VERSION

Tell them before the deadline, propose a new date, and hit that one.

WHY THIS IS HARDER FOR YOU

The instinct is to go silent and hope, and silence is what turns a small miss into a broken relationship. People forgive late far more easily than they forgive surprise.

The message before the deadline is worth ten apologies after it.

DO THIS

1. **Send the message as soon as you know,** not the night of.
2. **Do not explain at length.** I am not going to have this by Friday.
3. **Propose a specific new date** that you are confident about.
4. **Pad it.** Ask for more time than you think you need.
5. **Hit the new date without fail.** That is what preserves the trust.

IF IT GOES SIDEWAYS

If you have missed several deadlines with the same person, stop asking for extensions and start turning things in half finished on time. On time and partial usually beats late and complete.

102 HOW TO FILL OUT FORMS WITHOUT LOSING YOUR MIND

MOVE 02 · SHRINK THE FIRST STEP

MOVE 01 · GET IT OUT OF YOUR HEAD

THE TEN SECOND VERSION

Gather every document first, do it in one sitting, and save a copy.

WHY THIS IS HARDER FOR YOU

Forms fail for you in the middle, when you hit a field requiring a number you do not have, get up to find it, and never return.

Gathering everything first is the entire skill.

DO THIS

1. **Read the whole form before filling anything in.**
2. **Gather every document and number it asks for** and put them next to you.
3. **Do the whole form in one sitting,** even a boring one. Returning to a half done form rarely happens.
4. **Save or photograph the completed form** before you send it.
5. **Write the submission date and any confirmation number** in your notes.

> IF IT GOES SIDEWAYS
>
> *If a field stops you, put a placeholder and keep going. Finishing with one gap beats abandoning it at question four.*

103 HOW TO KEEP TRACK OF IMPORTANT DOCUMENTS

MOVE 04 · CHANGE THE ROOM

MOVE 01 · GET IT OUT OF YOUR HEAD

THE TEN SECOND VERSION

One folder, physical and digital. Photograph everything the day you get it.

WHY THIS IS HARDER FOR YOU

Birth certificate, Social Security card, ID, insurance card, diagnosis paperwork. You will need each of these at a moment when you have no time to find them.

Ten minutes of setup saves a genuinely terrible afternoon later.

DO THIS

1. **Get one physical folder** and put every original in it. One folder, one place.
2. **Photograph every document** and put the photos in one clearly named phone album or cloud folder.
3. **Never carry your Social Security card.** Keep it at home in the folder.
4. **Before you move out, get your own copies of five things:** birth certificate, Social Security card, photo ID, insurance card, and your diagnosis paperwork.
5. **Add anything new to both places the day you get it.**

IF IT GOES SIDEWAYS

If you have lost something important, replacing it is a form and a fee, not a catastrophe. Start with the issuing agency's website.

104 HOW TO EXPLAIN A GAP OR A BAD SEMESTER

MOVE 05 · SAY IT EARLY AND SHORT

THE TEN SECOND VERSION

One sentence of context, one sentence of what changed, then move forward.

WHY THIS IS HARDER FOR YOU

A bad stretch is not disqualifying, but a long defensive explanation makes it sound like it should be. People take their cue from how you deliver it.

Short and forward looking is what makes it land as history rather than a warning.

DO THIS

1. **Name it briefly and without drama.** I had a rough year in tenth grad
2. **Do not overshare the details.** Nobody needs the full account.
3. **Say what changed,** specifically. I got diagnosed and started using a system that works.
4. **Point at evidence since then.** Grades, attendance, a job you held.
5. **Change the subject to what you want now.**

> IF IT GOES SIDEWAYS
>
> *If you are asked repeatedly about it, answer the same short way each time. Consistency reads as honesty. Elaboration reads as anxiety.*

105 HOW TO FIND PEOPLE WHO GET IT

MOVE 06 · BORROW OUTSIDE STRUCTURE

THE TEN SECOND VERSION

Look for people who share the wiring, not just the interest.

WHY THIS IS HARDER FOR YOU

Being around other people with ADHD does something no amount of reading does. You stop explaining yourself constantly and find out that half of what you thought was personal is just common.

That shift is worth going looking for.

DO THIS

1. **Ask your counselor or doctor if a group exists locally.** Many schools and clinics run them.
2. **Look for interest based communities first,** where connection happens sideways rather than head on.
3. **Try one online space,** and leave any that mostly trade in despair.
4. **Say the thing out loud to one friend** and see what happens. It goes better than people expect.
5. **Notice who makes you feel normal** and spend more time with them.

> IF IT GOES SIDEWAYS
>
> *If a group is all complaining and no strategies, it is not helping. Find one that talks about what works.*

106 HOW TO ASK FOR HELP BEFORE IT IS AN EMERGENCY

MOVE 05 · SAY IT EARLY AND SHORT

MOVE 03 · BUILD IN A DELAY

THE TEN SECOND VERSION

Ask when it is a problem, not when it is a crisis. Name the specific help you want.

WHY THIS IS HARDER FOR YOU

You wait because asking feels like admitting something, and by the time you ask, the problem has grown teeth and the help required is much larger.

Early help is small. Late help is a project.

DO THIS

1. **Set a trigger in advance.** If I am two assignments behind, I ask.
2. **Pick one specific person** rather than hoping someone notices.
3. **Ask for something concrete.** Can you sit with me while I do this, or can I get two more days.
4. **Say the actual situation,** not a softened version. Softened versions get softened help.
5. **Ask again if the first person cannot help.** One no is not the answer, it is one person's answer.

IF IT GOES SIDEWAYS

If asking feels impossible, write it instead of saying it. A text counts. Getting the help is the point, not how it was delivered.

107 HOW TO HANDLE ADVICE FROM PEOPLE WHO DO NOT GET IT

MOVE 05 · SAY IT EARLY AND SHORT

THE TEN SECOND VERSION

Take the part that is useful, leave the rest, and do not run the debate.

WHY THIS IS HARDER FOR YOU

You will hear just try harder and everyone gets distracted for the rest of your life, usually from people who mean well and have no idea what they are describing.

Arguing about it costs you energy and changes almost nobody's mind.

DO THIS

1. **Say thanks and let it go** when the advice is useless but harmless.
2. **Take any part that is actually useful,** because sometimes there is one.
3. **Do not defend the diagnosis** to someone who is not going to move.
4. **Use one line if you need to:** that works for some people, this is what works for me.
5. **Save your energy for the people whose opinion actually affects your life,** like a teacher, a boss, or a parent.

> IF IT GOES SIDEWAYS
>
> *If it is a parent or a coach and it keeps happening, ask them to read one thing. A page from a book lands better than an argument.*

108 HOW TO BELIEVE YOU CAN ACTUALLY RUN YOUR OWN LIFE

MOVE 01 · GET IT OUT OF YOUR HEAD

THE TEN SECOND VERSION

Collect evidence. Write down what you handled, because your brain does not save those files.

WHY THIS IS HARDER FOR YOU

You have a very complete internal record of everything you have messed up and almost no record of what you have handled. That is not humility, it is a storage bias, and it makes you underestimate yourself constantly.

You have to build the other file manually.

DO THIS

1. **Keep a running list of things you handled.** Any size. A hard conversation, a deadline you hit, a job you got.
2. **Add to it weekly,** because you will not remember these later otherwise.
3. **Read it when you are convinced you cannot do something.** It is evidence, not encouragement.
4. **Notice which skills in this book you already use** without thinking about it anymore.
5. **Teach one of them to someone else.** Teaching is what turns a technique into something you own.

IF IT GOES SIDEWAYS

If the list feels short, start it today. Two weeks of writing things down will surprise you, and that surprise is the whole point.

109 HOW TO TALK TO A COACH OR BOSS WHO THINKS YOU ARE NOT TRYING

MOVE 05 · SAY IT EARLY AND SHORT

THE TEN SECOND VERSION

Do not argue with the verdict. Ask what it looks like when it is fixed.

WHY THIS IS HARDER FOR YOU

Effort is invisible and results are not, so people judge the one they can see. You have probably worked harder than anyone in the room and had it read as coasting.

Arguing about how hard you tried never once worked on anybody. Changing what they can see does.

DO THIS

1. **Ask for two minutes at a calm moment,** not right after a mistake and not in front of the group.
2. **Skip the defense entirely.** Do not open with I am trying, even though you are.
3. **Ask the useful question:** what would it look like to you if I was getting this right.
4. **Write down the answer in front of them.** Nothing signals seriousness faster, and it is free.
5. **Pick one thing off the list and do it visibly for two weeks,** then check back in with them once.

> IF IT GOES SIDEWAYS
>
> *If nothing you do changes their mind and it is not the only place you can be, spend your energy somewhere it lands. Some people made up their mind in week one.*

110 HOW TO FIX A BAD GRADE BEFORE IT BECOMES A BAD SEMESTER

MOVE 01 · GET IT OUT OF YOUR HEAD

MOVE 05 · SAY IT EARLY AND SHORT

THE TEN SECOND VERSION

Check the actual number, do the math on what is left, and email the teacher this week.

WHY THIS IS HARDER FOR YOU

A grade slide is silent. Nothing happens, nothing happens, nothing happens, and then it is week fourteen and the arithmetic no longer works no matter what you do.

The window where it is fixable is enormous and the window where it is not is small. You just cannot feel the difference from the inside.

DO THIS

1. **Open the grade portal and look at the real number today.** The number in your head is either kinder or crueler than the truth, never equal to it.
2. **Find what is actually costing you.** It is usually three missing assignments, not the tests. Missing zeros do more damage than bad scores.
3. **Do the math on what is left.** How much is still ungraded tells you whether this is a nudge or a rescue.
4. **Email the teacher this week** and ask what is still accepted and what would help most. Ask before the last two weeks, when everyone else asks.
5. **Put a portal check on the calendar every other Friday** so the next slide gets caught in week three instead of week fourteen.

IF IT GOES SIDEWAYS

If the math genuinely does not work anymore, go talk to your counselor about options now. There are usually more of them than you think, and all of them shrink as the term ends.

THE LAST THING

You are not going to use all hundred and one of these. Nobody does.

What actually happens is that four or five of them quietly become how you operate, and in two years you will not remember that they came from anywhere. That is the goal. A skill you have to think about is still work. A skill you just do is yours.

So pick one. Not five. One. Run it for two weeks, badly, missing days, coming back to it. Two weeks of a mediocre system beats a perfect system you abandoned on day three.

Then pick the next one.

One more thing worth saying plainly. Your brain is not a defective version of everyone else's. It is genuinely worse at some things, and the things it is worse at happen to be heavily rewarded in school. It is also genuinely better at some things, and most of those get rewarded later, in rooms where somebody has to notice the thing nobody else noticed, or care enormously about something for eleven hours straight.

School is a narrow test. You are not going to be in school forever.

You are going to be fine. Not organized, necessarily. Fine.

Go run your life.

EXAMPLES

Some skills are easier to copy than to describe. The next six pages are the finished versions.

None of these are impressive on purpose. The resume belongs to a kid who has never had a real job. The emails are four sentences. The scripts are shorter than you expect them to be.

That is the point. Copy the shape, swap in your own details, and stop trying to make it sound more important than it is.

A RESUME WITH NO JOB HISTORY

Everything on this one is school, sports, and side work. That is enough. Copy the shape, swap in your own.

MARCUS T. RIVERA

Austin, TX · (512) 555 0147 · marcus.t.rivera@email.com

EXPERIENCE

Lawn Care, Self Employed Summer 2024 to present

- Built a route of 11 regular customers through door to door outreach and referrals.
- Managed scheduling, invoicing, and equipment maintenance independently.
- Averaged $340 per month while carrying a full class schedule.

Babysitter 2023 to present

- Care for 3 children ages 4 to 9 for two families on a weekly schedule.
- Trusted with meals, homework help, and bedtime routines without supervision.

ACTIVITIES AND LEADERSHIP

Varsity Soccer, Lakeview High School 2023 to present

- Attended 100 percent of practices across two seasons.
- Elected team captain by teammates in junior year.

Food Bank Volunteer, Central Texas Food Bank 2024

- Completed 40 service hours sorting and packing donations.

SKILLS

- Fluent in English and Spanish, written and spoken.
- Cash handling, Google Workspace, basic small engine repair.
- Valid Texas driver license, clean record.

REFERENCES

- Available on request.

→One page. Always one page at this stage.

→Every line starts with a verb and includes a number where one exists. Numbers are what make it real.

→Attendance and reliability are worth listing. That is what a manager hiring a teenager is actually buying.

TWO EMAILS THAT GET ANSWERED

Both are under five sentences. Both name the ask by the second sentence. That is the whole formula.

ASKING A TEACHER FOR SOMETHING

Subject: Question about Thursday's chemistry test

Hi Ms. Delgado,

This is Marcus Rivera from your 4th period class. I have extended time as an accommodation and I wanted to ask where I should take Thursday's test so it is set up ahead of time.

Let me know what works and I will be there. Thank you.

Marcus Rivera

TELLING SOMEONE YOU WILL MISS A DEADLINE

Subject: Lab report, new date

Hi Mr. Okafor,

This is Marcus Rivera from 2nd period. I am not going to have the lab report finished by Friday. I can have it to you by Tuesday at the start of class.

Let me know if that works or if there is a different deadline I should hit. Thank you.

Marcus Rivera

→Notice what is missing from the second one: no explanation, no apology paragraph, no promise it will never happen again.

→A specific new date is what makes it a plan instead of an excuse.

→Send it before the deadline, not after. That single detail is most of why it works.

A PAY STUB, LINE BY LINE

Two weeks at $14 an hour. Check the top box against the bottom box every single time.

WESTGATE MARKET · Pay period 03/01 to 03/14 · Pay date 03/20			
EARNINGS	HOURS	RATE	AMOUNT
Regular	62.00	$14.00	$868.00
Overtime	2.00	$21.00	$42.00
Gross pay			**$910.00**
DEDUCTIONS			AMOUNT
Federal income tax			$61.40
Social Security			$56.42
Medicare			$13.20
Net pay			**$778.98**

- →Multiply hours by rate yourself. 62 x $14 is $868. If that number is off, your hours are wrong and you tell your manager this week.
- →Overtime is time and a half. $14 becomes $21 past 40 hours in a week.
- →Texas has no state income tax, so there is no line for it here. Most states do have one and it will sit under federal.
- →Net pay is what actually lands in your account. Gross pay is the number you tell people. Budget with net.

THE SPLIT, WITH REAL NUMBERS

Same $778.98 from the pay stub, moved the day it lands. Nothing here requires you to remember anything mid month.

WHERE IT GOES	PERCENT	AMOUNT
Spending account	50%	$389.49
Savings account	30%	$233.69
Bills account	20%	$155.80
Total	**100%**	**$778.98**

WHAT EACH ONE IS FOR

- **Spending.** Food out, games, clothes, anything you want. When it is gone, it is gone until the next check. This is the only account you touch.
- **Savings.** Named for a goal, like Car or Move Out. Kept at a different bank so a transfer takes a day.
- **Bills.** Phone, subscriptions, insurance. Autopay pulls from here so nothing depends on you remembering.

IF THE NUMBERS DO NOT FIT

- Keep the three accounts and change the percentages. 70 / 20 / 10 still works. Three accounts with bad percentages beats one account with a perfect plan.

→Do the split the day the money lands, not the weekend after. The weekend after is where it disappears.

→Automate the transfers if your bank lets you, and the whole system runs without you.

YOUR THREE INTERVIEW STORIES

Fill these in before you go. Almost every interview question is one of these three wearing a different hat.

STORY 1: A TIME YOU SOLVED A PROBLEM

Example: A customer's order got lost on a busy Saturday. I found the ticket, remade it myself, and told my manager before the customer had to ask twice.

YOURS:

STORY 2: A TIME YOU WORKED WITH SOMEONE DIFFICULT

Example: A group project partner stopped responding. I finished my part, documented what was missing, and told the teacher before the due date instead of after.

YOURS:

STORY 3: A TIME YOU WERE RELIABLE

Example: I made every soccer practice for two seasons, including the ones at six in the morning in January.

YOURS:

- →Keep each story to about thirty seconds spoken. Say it out loud once before you go, in the car.
- →End every story with what happened as a result. That is the part interviewers are listening for.
- →If you get a question you did not prepare for, pick the closest story and use it. Nobody is checking.

FOUR SCRIPTS FOR HARD SENTENCES

These are short on purpose. Every extra sentence gives the other person somewhere to argue.

ASKING FOR A RAISE

Do you have five minutes sometime this week? I have been here eight months, I close on my own now, and I trained two new people. I would like to move to fifteen an hour.

Then stop talking. Let the silence sit.

SAYING NO TO A FRIEND

I cannot make it.

That is the whole thing. No reason attached, because reasons can be argued with.

APOLOGIZING

I was forty minutes late and I did not text you. That was on me. I am setting an alarm for next time.

Name it, say what changes, stop. No explanation of why.

TELLING SOMEONE YOU HAVE ADHD

I have ADHD. It mostly means I lose track of time and I need things in writing. If you text me plans, put the time in the text.

Two sentences and one specific ask. Then change the subject.

→Read each one out loud once. Sentences you have said before come out steadier than sentences you are inventing.

→In all four, the silence after you finish is doing work. Do not fill it.

SKILLS BY MOVE

If one of the six works for your brain, here is everything else that runs on it.

01 GET IT OUT OF YOUR HEAD

04 Break a Huge Assignment Into Pieces You Will Actually Start · 05 Use a Calendar That Survives Real Life · 06 Remember Something Without Writing It Down Badly · 08 Estimate How Long Something Will Really Take · 11 Pack for a Trip Without Forgetting Something Important · 13 Follow Multi Step Instructions Without Losing Step Three · 22 Take Notes You Will Actually Use Later · 26 Stop Paying for Subscriptions You Forgot About · 29 Write a Resume With No Work Experience · 30 Get Through a Job Interview · 32 Read a Pay Stub · 37 Understand What Insurance Actually Is · 42 Move Out With Money That Actually Works · 44 Stop Interrupting Without Losing Your Thought · 50 Keep a Friendship You Keep Forgetting to Maintain · 57 Be a Good Partner When You Forget Things · 63 Be Someone People Can Count On · 67 Fall Asleep When Your Brain Will Not Stop · 77 Go to a Doctor Appointment and Actually Get What You Need · 80 Deal With a Racing Mind During the Day · 90 Understand Your Own Accommodations · 97 Get Accommodations in College · 102 Fill Out Forms Without Losing Your Mind · 103 Keep Track of Important Documents · 108 Believe You Can Actually Run Your Own Life · 110 Fix a Bad Grade Before It Becomes a Bad Semester

02 SHRINK THE FIRST STEP

02 Start Homework When Your Brain Says No · 04 Break a Huge Assignment Into Pieces You Will Actually Start · 09 Handle a Sudden Schedule Change Without Losing the Day · 12 Finish Something You Are Ninety Percent Done With · 14 Stop Reading the Same Paragraph Six Times · 19 Recover a Day That Fell Apart by Noon · 28 Find a First Job · 70 Learn Five Meals You Can Make · 72 Move Your Body When the Gym Is Overwhelming · 74 Manage a Day With No Motivation · 91 Study for a Test When Reviewing Is Boring · 92 Pass the Written Driving Test · 95 Set a Goal You Will Still Care About in Three Weeks · 96 Decide What to Do After High School · 102 Fill Out Forms Without Losing Your Mind

03 BUILD IN A DELAY

01 Get Out the Door on Time · 15 Wait Without Losing Your Mind · 18 Stop Saying Yes to Everything · 21 Stop a Game From Eating Your Entire Saturday · 24 Budget When You Spend Impulsively · 25 Use the Twenty Four Hour Rule · 30 Get Through a Job Interview · 34 Avoid Buy Now

04 CHANGE THE ROOM

05 SAY IT EARLY AND SHORT

06 BORROW OUTSIDE STRUCTURE

FIND IT FAST

When you do not know what you need but you know how you feel.

I CANNOT MAKE MYSELF START

Start homework when your brain says no. Break a huge assignment into pieces. Body doubling.

I AM ALWAYS LATE

Get out the door on time. Estimate how long something will really take. Use a calendar that survives real life.

I KEEP LOSING THINGS

Stop losing your keys, wallet, and phone. Keep a room you can find things in. Keep track of important documents.

I AM BROKE AND I DO NOT KNOW WHY

Budget when you spend impulsively. Stop paying for subscriptions you forgot. Track spending without a complicated app.

I WANT TO BUY SOMETHING RIGHT NOW

The twenty four hour rule. Say no to a purchase your friends are making. Avoid buy now pay later traps.

I NEED A JOB

Find a first job. Write a resume with no work experience. Get through a job interview.

I SAID SOMETHING WRONG

Apologize without over apologizing. Read a room when you missed the cue. Stop interrupting.

SOMEBODY IS UPSET WITH ME

Take criticism without shutting down. Disagree without it turning into a fight. Have a hard conversation with your parents.

NOBODY HAS TEXTED ME BACK

Text without spiraling over a read receipt. Handle rejection sensitivity in the moment. Handle being left out.

I HAVE NO FRIENDS HERE

Make a friend when you are new. Keep a friendship you forget to maintain. Find people who get it.

I CANNOT SLEEP

Fall asleep when your brain will not stop. Get off your phone at night. Get yourself outside every day.

I FEEL AWFUL AND I DO NOT KNOW WHY

Notice what your body is telling you. Manage a day with no motivation. Handle being overstimulated.

I HAVE NOT EATEN TODAY

Eat when cooking feels impossible. Learn five meals you can make.

I FORGOT TO TAKE MY MEDS AGAIN

Take medication consistently. Go to a doctor appointment and get what you need.

I FAILED SOMETHING

Recover from failing something. Handle a deadline you are going to miss. Explain a gap or a bad semester.

I NEED SOMETHING FROM A TEACHER

Ask a teacher for what you need. Write an email an adult will take seriously. Understand your own accommodations.

I AM ABOUT TO BE ON MY OWN

Manage yourself with no one checking on you. Get accommodations in college. Move out with money that works.

A GAME JUST ATE MY WHOLE DAY

Stop a game from eating your entire Saturday. Handle being bored without wrecking something.

I JUST BLEW UP AT SOMEBODY

Catch anger before it runs the room. Come back after you blew up at your parents.

EVERYONE ONLINE IS DOING BETTER THAN ME

Stop comparing yourself to everyone on your phone. Handle being left out.

MY SIBLING IS IMPOSSIBLE

Live with a sibling who knows every button. Disagree without it turning into a fight.

MY GRADE DROPPED AND I AM SCARED TO LOOK

Fix a bad grade before it becomes a bad semester. Talk to a coach or boss who thinks you are not trying.

SOMETHING ONLINE FEELS OFF

Not get scammed online. Avoid buy now pay later traps.

I AM BEING HARD ON MYSELF

Be decent to yourself about all of this. Believe you can run your own life. Know when something bigger is going on.

REFERENCES

The pages in this book that make claims about how ADHD brains work are drawn from the research below. Where a claim is about a general pattern rather than a single study, the entry points to the review or meta-analysis that summarizes it.

ON ADHD, SUBSTANCE USE, AND NICOTINE

Charach, A., Yeung, E., Climans, T., & Lillie, E. (2011). Childhood attention-deficit/hyperactivity disorder and future substance use disorders: Comparative meta-analyses. *Journal of the American Academy of Child & Adolescent Psychiatry, 50*(1), 9 to 21.

Lee, S. S., Humphreys, K. L., Flory, K., Liu, R., & Glass, K. (2011). Prospective association of childhood attention-deficit/hyperactivity disorder and substance use and abuse/dependence: A meta-analytic review. *Clinical Psychology Review, 31*(3), 328 to 341.

Groenman, A. P., et al. (2013). Substance use disorders in adolescents with attention deficit hyperactivity disorder: A 4-year follow-up study. *Addiction, 108*(8), 1503 to 1511.

McCabe, S. E., et al. (2025). Attention-deficit/hyperactivity disorder symptoms and later e-cigarette and tobacco use in US youth. Reported in *MGB Psychiatry News*, April 2025.

ON CANNABIS AND THE DEVELOPING BRAIN

Scott, J. C., Slomiak, S. T., Jones, J. D., Rosen, A. F. G., Moore, T. M., & Gur, R. C. (2018). Association of cannabis with cognitive functioning in adolescents and young adults: A systematic review and meta-analysis. *JAMA Psychiatry, 75*(6), 585 to 595.

Dellazizzo, L., et al. (2022). Evidence on the acute and residual neurocognitive effects of cannabis use in adolescents and adults: A systematic meta-review of meta-analyses. *Addiction, 117*(7), 1857 to 1870.

ON DRIVING

Meta-analyses of driving outcomes in ADHD report risk of negative driving events roughly 1.2 to 1.9 times higher than in drivers without ADHD, with untreated ADHD showing the largest effect. See the systematic review and meta-analysis of untreated ADHD and motor vehicle accidents published in *Advances in Therapy* (2026).

ON EXERCISE

Systematic reviews and network meta-analyses of randomized controlled trials consistently find that physical exercise improves core ADHD symptoms and executive function in children and adolescents. See the network meta-analysis in *Frontiers in Psychology* (2023) covering 59 studies, and the three-level meta-analysis of 42 randomized controlled trials in *Adolescent Research Review* (2026).

ON SLEEP

Meta-analytic reviews find that adolescents with ADHD report significantly worse subjective sleep and more sleep problems than peers without ADHD, and that delayed melatonin onset and misaligned sleep-wake cycles are common. See the systematic review and meta-analysis of sleep parameters in adolescents with and without ADHD (2023) and subsequent narrative reviews of sleep disturbance in ADHD.

GENERAL READING

Barkley, R. A. *Taking Charge of ADHD: The Complete, Authoritative Guide for Parents.* Guilford Press.

Hallowell, E. M., & Ratey, J. J. *ADHD 2.0: New Science and Essential Strategies for Thriving with Distraction.* Ballantine Books.

CHADD, Children and Adults with Attention-Deficit/Hyperactivity Disorder. chadd.org

National Institute of Mental Health. Attention-Deficit/Hyperactivity Disorder. nimh.nih.gov

ABOUT THE AUTHOR

RICHARD BASS

Richard Bass is a certified special education teacher and bestselling author with over a decade of experience supporting children and teens with neurodivergence, anxiety, and depression.

He holds bachelor's and master's degrees in education, with certifications in Special Education, kindergarten through twelfth grade, and Educational Administration.

He has written over 30 books and workbooks on ADHD, autism, ODD, and social and emotional learning, with more than 100,000 copies sold. His flagship title, *The ADHD Parenting Guide for Boys*, is a Mom's Choice Gold Award winner available in four languages.

He has spent his career in classrooms with the kids this book is written for: bright, funny, capable boys who kept being told they were not trying, when the truth was that nobody had shown them a system built for the brain they actually have.

This book is the set of systems he wishes somebody had handed them at thirteen.

Free resources. Richard shares strategies, walkthroughs, and encouragement on his YouTube channel, **Thriving with Richard Bass**.

If this book helped, a review helps another kid find it. It takes about a minute and it matters more than you would think.

ALSO BY RICHARD BASS

WORKBOOKS FOR TEENS

THE TEENS' WORKBOOK TO SELF REGULATE

Empowering Teenagers to Handle Emotions with Success through Coping Strategies and CBT Exercises.

THE TEENS' WORKBOOK TO SELF REGULATE: ADVANCED EDITION

Mastering Emotional Intelligence Through Advanced CBT Techniques and Resilience Building.

THE DBT WORKBOOK FOR TEENS

Mindfulness and Emotion Regulation Techniques for Overcoming Stress and Negative Thoughts.

BEYOND COPING SKILLS: THE ULTIMATE TEENS' WORKBOOK

Integrating CBT and DBT for Lasting Emotional Regulation and Personal Growth.

THE INNER STRENGTH WORKBOOK FOR TEENS

Stop Self-Doubt, Start Self-Love. Practical exercises to build confidence and overcome comparison.

MORE FOR TEENS

NEURODIVERGENT TEENS

Twelve success stories of teens with ADHD and autism who learned to thrive, with proven strategies and weekly action plans.

THE INTO GROWTH SERIES

Four seasonal social and emotional learning workbooks for teens, thirty five exercises apiece.

SOCIAL EMOTIONAL LEARNING WORKBOOK FOR HIGH SCHOOL

Navigating Emotions with Grade Level Activities.

FOR THE ADULTS RAISING THEM

THE ADHD PARENTING GUIDE FOR GIRLS

For the adult raising a daughter with ADHD.

THE ADHD PARENTING GUIDE FOR BOYS

Mom's Choice Gold Award winner, available in four languages. The companion to this book, written for the adult on the other side of the same house.

Over thirty titles in print on ADHD, autism, ODD, and social and emotional learning, for children, tweens, teens, and the adults raising them.

Find them all at richardbassauthor.com

THINGS I HANDLED

Skill 110 says to keep a list of things you handled, because your brain does not save those files on its own. Start it here. Any size counts.